THE YEAR I WAS BORN

Compiled by Felicity Trotman

Signpost Books

Published by Signpost Books, Ltd
25 Eden Drive, Headington, Oxford OX3 0AB

First published 1995
10987654321

Based on an original idea by Sally Wood
Conceived, designed and produced by Signpost Books, Ltd

Compiler: Felicity Trotman
Designer: Paul Fry
Editor: Dorothy Wood

ISBN 1 874785 25 2

Acknowledgments: Mirror Group Newspapers plc. for all the pictures in which they hold copyright, and Hugh Gallacher for his invaluable help in retrieving them from the files; Associated Press, pp. 32-33, 60, 61, 70, 71, 83; Camera Press, p. 68; Faber & Faber, pp. 30, 31; Hulton Deutsch Collection, pp. 34, 51, 86, 87; National Portrait Gallery p. 10. Range/Bettman/UPI pp. 73. 87, 95.
Every effort has been made to trace all copyright holders, but if any have been inadvertently overlooked, the publishers will be pleased to make the necessary arrangements at the first opportunity.

Printed and bound in Italy.

Cover pictures: (Front, clockwise, from top) Prince Rainier of Monaco marries actress Grace Kelly; Students warn against war during the Suez Crisis; Premium Bonds are launched; Devon Loch falters in the final strides of the Grand National; Russian tanks roll in to quell unrest in Budapest, Hungary.

ME THEN

ME NOW

PERSONAL PROFILE

Names:

Date of Birth:

Place of Birth: Time of Birth:

Weight at Birth: Parents' names:

Colour of Eyes: Colour of Hair:

Distinguishing Marks: Weight now:

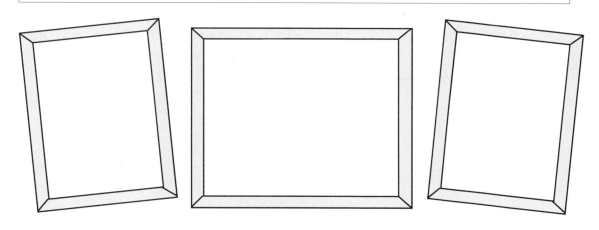

MY FAMILY

1 Sunday
New Year's Day

New Year's Honours: Professor Solly Zuckerman becomes a Knight Bachelor: Margot Fonteyn is awarded the DBE, and CBEs go to **Douglas Bader** *(left, with his wife)*, Agatha Christie, L P Hartley, Sir Osbert Sitwell and C V Wedgewood.

■ All newspapers in China will be printed in horizontal script, not vertical, and will be read from left to right.
■ 112 people are killed and at least 75 injured after a steep stone staircase leading to a Shinto shrine at Yashiko, 160 miles north of Tokyo, Japan, collapses.
■ Britain and the USA agree to help fund the **Aswan High Dam** project in Egypt.

2 Monday

Dr Michael Ramsay (51, *below*), the Bishop of Durham, is to be the new Archbishop of York.
. . . General election in France . . .
■ The Diocese of Rochester gives permission for the opening of Sir Thomas Walsingham's tomb in Chislehurst, Kent. It may contain manuscripts proving that Christopher Marlowe wrote Shakespeare's plays.

3 Tuesday

Sir Winston Churchill has accepted the honorary appointment as Grand Seigneur of The Hudson's Bay Company, the oldest chartered trading company in the world.
■ Fire breaks out in a TV relay post, 850ft up on 3rd floor of the **Eiffel Tower**. Firemen have to carry all their equipment up as the lifts can't be used. The fire is extinguished in about 2 hours.

4 Wednesday

An American practice bomb, released by mistake from a B47 aircraft, explodes in a ploughed field at Newport, Essex, leaving a crater 15ft deep and damaging greenhouses in neighbouring nurseries. A USAF spokesman says the bomb was completely inert, and the crew did not realise it had been released.

5 Thursday

The entire population of the village of Enford, Wilts, is prosecuted at the Quarter Sessions in Devizes for allowing part of the common highway to go out of repair. The case has been brought to decide if the County Council is liable to make up the highway. The villagers are found guilty.
■ **Prince Rainier III** of Monaco (32) announces his engagement to film actress **Grace Kelly** (26).
■ Fog covers the country from the south coast to Yorkshire, causing the worst driving conditions since 1952.
■ **Mistinguett**, (real name Jeanne Marie Bourgeois) French singer and entertainer, dies from a heart attack and pneumonia at her home in France.

6 Friday

Mrs Odette Churchill, GC, famous wartime secret agent, marries. *(See panel, opposite)*
■ The fog continues. 200 babies between 6-12 months old have been taken to hospital in Liverpool with bronchial pneumonia since Christmas: a virus aggravated by fog.

7 Saturday

George Lockhart, ringmaster at the Belle Vue International Circus, Manchester, is severely bitten by an elephant, Burma (4 tons). The elephant seizes Mr Lockhart's left arm in his mouth and crushes it. Mr Lockhart gives Burma a chocolate and goes on with the

Terrorists Stalk Cyprus in Violent Power Struggle

Following the declaration of a State of Emergency at the end of last year, Greek Cypriots continue their campaign of civil disobedience and terror to further their demands for *ENOSIS* – union with Greece. The banned EOKA terrorists employ bombs and assassinations against civilian and military targets alike. After talks with Archbishop Makarios break down, he is arrested as a terrorist and deported to the Seychelles. Appeal court judge Lord Radcliffe arrives in Cyprus in the summer for consultations before drawing up a new constitution which, it is hoped, will lead to independence for Cyprus.

Top left: **A 22-year-old Cypriot girl gazes in horror at the body of her Maltese fiancé, who has been shot down in a Nicosia street. In a broadcast interview, she calls on Grivas, the rebel leader, to 'get out of our land'.** *Bottom left:* **Archbishop Makarios just before he is arrested.** *Centre:* **This Greek Cypriot is shot dead outside a cinema.** *Bottom right:* **The taxi driver is the victim of another terrorist outrage.**

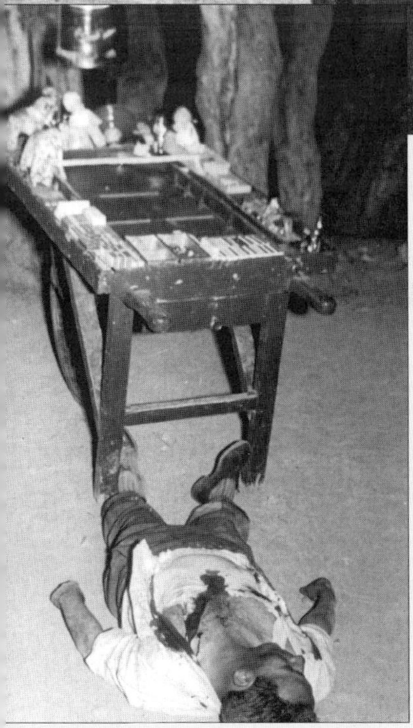

■ The *Theron* is free, after being ice-bound for more than 4 weeks in the Weddell Sea. She's trying to reach Vahsel Bay, Antarctica – a voyage of about 1,200 miles – to establish a base.
■ New Zealand calls for **Antarctica** to be placed under UN trusteeship, and declared an area where peaceful citizens of any nation would have equal privileges.

25 Wednesday

A demonstration takes place in New York of a new technique for amplifying light. The **Lumicon** can increase the brightness of an image 50,000 times. It has already been used at the Lowell Observatory, Flagstaff, Arizona, to produce the best-ever pictures of **Mars**.
■ British troops are stoned by schoolchildren at Paphos, **Cyprus**, and use tear-gas to disperse the crowd.
■ Mr Turton, Minister of Health, says the government supports the Guillebaud Committee's report on the cost of the National Health Service, and feels that it is not the time to make any fundamental alteration to its structure.

26 Thursday
Foundation Day, Australia

19,000 staff on **London Underground** get a pay rise and better working conditions. They will receive the same increase as British Rail staff – 7%, backdated to last Monday.
■ A new clause in the Road Traffic Bill provides for cars to be tested to ensure that they are in a satisfactory condition. **Driving licences** will run for 3yrs and cost 15s.
. . . The import and export of HEROIN is banned . . .

27 Friday
Full Moon

300 schoolboys in Nicosia, **Cyprus**, egged on by two Greek Cypriot priests, use iron bars and sticks to attack British troops. The soldiers use tear gas and batons to restore order. 30 children are slightly hurt.
■ The Queen and the Duke of Edinburgh leave London Airport for a **State visit to Nigeria**. They are given a rousing send-off from London airport by many Nigerians living in Britain. (See panel, opposite).
■ The River Severn is 15ft 3in above normal in Shrewsbury, Salop, and overflows its banks.

28 Saturday

France beat Ireland 14-8 in the rugby international at Stade des Colombes, Paris.
■ Seven men with shotguns try to get rid of the starlings roosting at the ICI ammonia works at Billingham on Tees, Co Durham, but are unsuccessful. The Deputy Manager says they'll keep on trying, with double the number of gunmen.
■ H L Mencken, American author, editor, and critic, dies aged 75. His classic work is *The American Language*.

29 Sunday

The Queen and the Duke of Edinburgh receive an enthusiastic welcome in Lagos at the start of their 3-week official visit to **Nigeria**. Carter Bridge, leading from Lagos Island to the mainland, is packed with 10,000 schoolchildren – whose weight had previously been assessed at 25 tons per 1,000 children!
■ The Indian government deny 'alarmist' reports about the state of the

FAREWELL TO A A MILNE, CREATOR OF POOH BEAR

DATELINE: January 31
A A Milne (74), playwright and author, best known for his children's classics *Winnie the Pooh, The House at Pooh Corner, When We were Very Young,* **etc. dies at his home in Hartfield, Sussex.**

Queen Delights in Tour of Nigeria

THE QUEEN and Prince Philip receive a rapturous welcome on their three-week State visit to Nigeria. Thousands line the streets of the capital, Lagos, to salute the royal couple. During the tour, the Queen receives a loyal address in the Nigerian Parliament – the only building with air-conditioning – and presents new colours to the 2nd Battalion Nigeria Regiment. She also visits the historic port of Calabar, where she meets the Obang of Calabar, Ededem Arhibon V (85), who wears an ivory crown and a necklet of leopards' fangs.

Taj Mahal. Rumours started when scaffolding was put up to repair a turret. Over £30,000 has been spent on repairs in the last 10yrs.

■ The Pan-Cyprian gymnasium in Nicosia, **Cyprus**, which has 2,000 pupils, is closed indefinitely for failing to maintain discipline.

30 Monday

The Sudan objects to Egypt's projected High Dam at **Aswan** which, they say, will flood Sudanese territory. Sudan also wants a new agreement on the division of the waters of the Nile, and Egypt to pay for the moving and rehousing of the 50,000 Sudanese who would be affected by dam.

■ **Lew Hoad** wins the Australian singles championship for the first time. He beats his partner and compatriot Ken Rosewall, 6-4, 3-6, 6-4, 7-5.

31 Tuesday

The LCC agree to put a blue plaque at 20, Maresfield Gardens, NW3. where **Sigmund Freud** lived after he fled Nazi-occupied Austria.

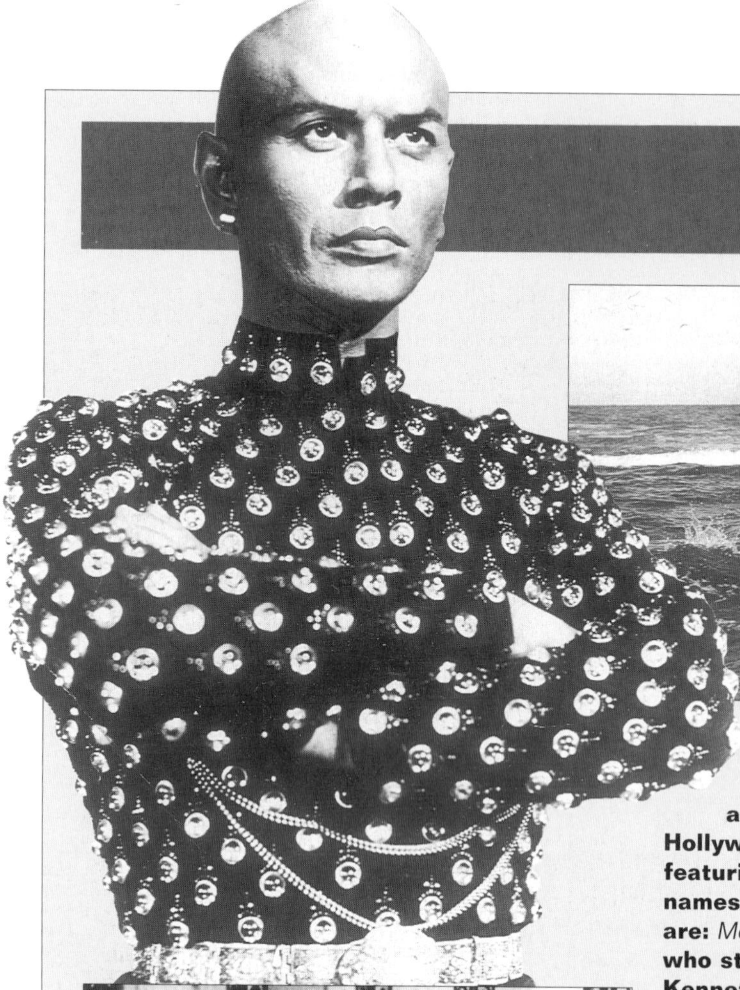

FILMS O

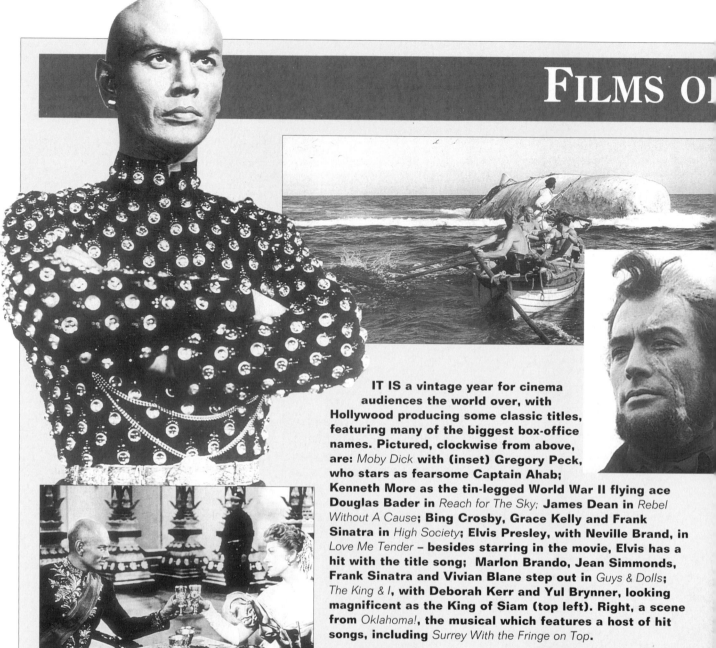

IT IS a vintage year for cinema audiences the world over, with Hollywood producing some classic titles, featuring many of the biggest box-office names. Pictured, clockwise from above, are: *Moby Dick* **with (inset) Gregory Peck, who stars as fearsome Captain Ahab; Kenneth More as the tin-legged World War II flying ace Douglas Bader in** *Reach for The Sky;* **James Dean in** *Rebel Without A Cause*; **Bing Crosby, Grace Kelly and Frank Sinatra in** *High Society*; **Elvis Presley, with Neville Brand, in** *Love Me Tender* **– besides starring in the movie, Elvis has a hit with the title song; Marlon Brando, Jean Simmonds, Frank Sinatra and Vivian Blane step out in** *Guys & Dolls*; *The King & I*, **with Deborah Kerr and Yul Brynner, looking magnificent as the King of Siam (top left). Right, a scene from** *Oklahoma!*, **the musical which features a host of hit songs, including** *Surrey With the Fringe on Top*.

THE YEAR

THE RAINS OF RANCHIPUR – Richard Burton, Michael Rennie, Lana Turner
THE MAN WHO NEVER WAS – Clifton Webb Robert Flemyng, André Morell,
YIELD TO THE NIGHT - Diana Dors, Yvonne Mitchell, Athene Seyler
THE MAN IN THE GREY FLANNEL SUIT – Gregory Peck
THE TENDER TRAP – Frank Sinatra, Doris Day
THE KING AND I – Yul Brynner, Deborah Kerr
BHOWANI JUNCTION – Ava Gardner
GUYS AND DOLLS – Frank Sinatra, Marlon Brando, Jean Simmonds
REBEL WITHOUT A CAUSE – James Dean
ROCK AROUND THE CLOCK – Bill Hailey & his Comets
A TOWN LIKE ALICE – Peter Finch, Virginia McKenna, Gordon Jackson
REACH FOR THE SKY – Kenneth More
OKLAHOMA! – Gordon Macrea, Rod Steiger, Shirley Jones
THE MAN WHO KNEW TOO MUCH – Doris Day, James Stewart
1984 – Edmund O'Brien, Jan Sterling, Michale Redgrave
FRIENDLY PERSUASION – Anthony Perkins
HIGH SOCIETY – Grace Kelly, Frank Sinatra, Bing Crosby, Celeste Holm
THE BATTLE OF THE RIVER PLATE – Peter Finch
LOVE ME TENDER – Elvis Presley
MOBY DICK – Gregory Peck, Orson Welles, Richard Basehart
WAR AND PEACE – Audrey Hepburn, Rod Steiger
SMILES OF A SUMMER NIGHT – Ulla Jacobsson, Eva Dahlbeck

■ Snow falls in most of Britain. The temperature in London at 11.00 pm was 24°F. Sheffield has its coldest day since 1947 – the needle never rises above 28°F.

FEBRUARY

1 Wednesday

A black **goat** found wandering in Linacre Road, Bootle, is taken by the RSPCA to spend the night in a Liverpool dog's home. Police circulate its description with the missing persons list to try to find the owner.

■ The finest **diamond** ever found in South Africa, an ice-blue stone weighing 426 carats, is delivered to its new owners, Harry Winston, Inc, in New York – wrapped in a brown paper bag. The messenger had no special guards.

■ The maximum temperature at Kew is 24.1°F. It's the coldest day since the Great Frost of February, 1895, when Kew's maximum temperature reached 23.1°F. It's 10°F in Birmingham and the **sea freezes** at Pegwell Bay, Kent.

2 Thursday

An **explosion** in two transformers blacks out 2sq miles of Liverpool and causes a fire at a Merseyside and North Wales Electricity Board substation. No ferries to Ireland can leave Waterloo Dock, because the power failure affects the hydro-electrically operated lock gates.

■ Dr H E Edgerton of the Massachusetts Institute of Technology in Boston, USA, has invented a **camera** which can take photos under water, and withstand pressures of 17,000 lb a sq in. – greater pressure than in the Challenger depths off Guam, the deepest known place in the oceans.

■ More than 1,000 standpipes are erected in London streets, as so many homes are without water because their pipes are frozen.

3 Friday

About 3,000 schoolchildren in Birmingham are sent home because it is too cold to work. nine schools close in Bournemouth, and 20 in Somerset.

■ At an agricultural show in Berlin, a 15ft pike leaps out of his pond and heads purposefully towards a stuffed hare. Attendants have great difficulty getting him back into his pond.

■ A Norwegian freighter, the *Dovrefjell* (9,750 tons) is stranded on the rocks of the Pentland Skerries, at the entrance to the Pentland Firth. The entire crew of 42 is rescued by helicopter.

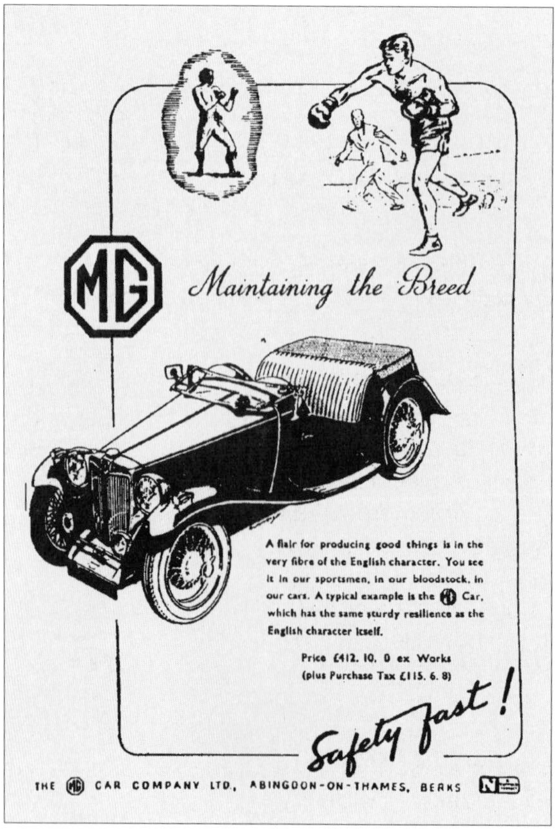

4 Saturday

Fourteen Football League matches are postponed because of snow, ice and frost.

■ East Berlin police cross into the American sector and try to abduct a former colleague who had sought **political asylum**. He's chased at pistol point into a service station, where he fights off an East German policeman. His sister-in-law stops police from snatching his children by throwing herself on top of them and screaming for help.

5 Sunday

The final day of the Winter Olympics.

■ No end in sight for the

1956 FACT FILE

World Population	**2,528,000,000 (est)**
World's Largest City (in population)	**New York 12,300,000 (Pop. 8,346,137 in 1951 Census)**
UK Population (males)	**24 773,000**
UK Population (females)	**256,447,000**
Population of London	**8,346,137**
Total UK Population	**51,221,000**
Total UK Area	**89,034,200 square miles**
Total London area	**616.4 square miles**
Head of State	**Queen Elizabeth II**
Prime Minister:	**Sir Anthony Eden MP**
House of Commons	**Conservatives 345 seats, Labour 277, Liberals 6, Sinn Fein 2, (declared invalid).**
Astronomer Royal	**Sir Harold Spencer Jones**
Poet Laureate	**John Edward Masefield**
Royal Swan Keeper	**F T Turk**
UK Births	**823,100**
UK Deaths	**597,900**
UK Marriages	**406,300**
UK Divorces	**29,788**
Licensed motor vehicles	**6,984,651**
TV licences	**5,812,178**
Emigration to Australia	**32,400**
Emigration to Canada	**43,400**
Emigration to New Zealand	**11,500**
Total UK Emigration	**116,700**
Total UK Immigration	**58,200**

The Council of Europe - Belgium, Denmark, France, Irish Republic, Italy, Luxembourg, The Netherlands, Norway, Sweden, UK, Turkey, Greece, Iceland, Saar, German Federal Republic.

NATO - North Atlantic Treaty Organization: Belgium, Canada, Denmark, Federal German Republic, France, Great Britain Greece, Iceland, Italy, Luxembourg, the Netherlands, Norway, Portugal, Turkey, USA

Australian **dock strike**. In Victoria alone butter is piling up at the rate of more than 4 million lbs a week. Abattoirs have shut because the cold stores are full.

■ A sudden rise in temperature – it's 53°F in Ventnor and Teignmouth – starts a thaw which causes **floods:** 1,200 burst pipes are reported in Walsall, and there are 2,000 emergency calls in Liverpool in 24hrs.

6 Monday

Autherine Lucy, the first black student at the University of Alabama, USA, is pelted with eggs by an angry crowd in Tuscaloosa. It's the third time there have been protests since she was admitted to the University under a Federal Court Order.

■ The Pan Cyprian Gymnasium in Famagusta is closed until further notice after 1,000 children riot. 15 out of 35 Greek secondary schools in Cyprus are now closed.

7 Tuesday

The **Elephant and Castle** area in London, which was badly bombed during World War II, is to be converted into the main 'commercial,

BOOKS OF THE YEAR

THE TRIBE THAT LOST ITS HEAD	Nicholas Monsarrat
HMS ULYSSES	Alistair MacLean
THE LAST OF THE WINE	Mary Renault
THE RETURN OF THE KING	J R R Tolkien
THE MARY DEARE	Hammond Innes
THE TOWERS OF TREBIZOND	Rose Macauley
THE QUIET AMERICAN	Graham Greene
ANGLO-SAXON ATTITUDES	Angus Wilson
A CERTAIN SMILE	François Sagan
FRENCH LEAVE	P G Wodehouse
A HISTORY OF THE ENGLISH-SPEAKING PEOPLES Vol 1 The Birth of Britain	Sir Winston Churchill
GALLIPOLI	Alan Moorhead
ZOO QUEST TO GUIANA	David Attenborough
NAUGHT FOR YOUR COMFORT	Trevor Huddlestone
A NIGHT TO REMEMBER	Walter Lord
MY FAMILY AND OTHER ANIMALS	Gerald Durrell

Top Authors: (clockwise from top left) François Sagan; Nicholas Monsarrat; Hammond Innes; J R R Tolkien; and, below, left, David Attenborough; below right Gerald Durrell.

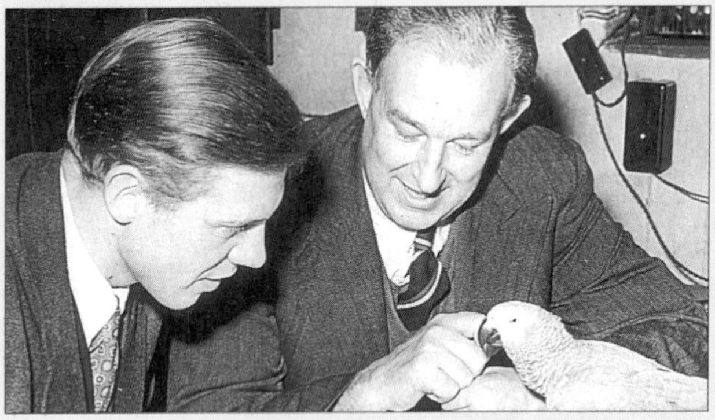

shopping and entertainment centre' of South London.

■ Keats, a 4-yr-old **Persian cat**, is chosen to take the feline role in a forthcoming production of *School for Fathers* at Sadlers Wells.There were 25 applications for the job, but 7 cats failed to arrive for their auditions.

. . . Prof. Henri Chrétien (77), the man who invented the lenses used in CINEMASCOPE cameras and projectors, dies in Washington, USA . . .

8 Wednesday

A new London bus, the **Routemaster**, goes into service on route 2 between Golders Green and Crystal Palace. It can carry 64 passengers, and will gradually replace existing buses and trolley buses.

■ Technicians from 25 countries meet in Geneva to try and standardize colour TV, so that programmes can be exchanged round the world.

■ The Queen visits the historic port of Calabar, Nigeria.

■ Because of an argument over the copyright, this year's Grand National will not be televised. It will, however, be broadcast on radio as usual.

9 Thursday

The Antarctic survey ship *Theron* is on her

way home earlier than expected because the weather is getting worse. Eight men remain at Shackleton Base to complete the building of the wooden hut in which they will spend the winter.
■ **Autherine Lucy** (see Feb 6) asks the Federal Court to readmit her to classes at the **University of Alabama**. She has been barred after 3 days of demonstrations.
. . . Frost and SNOW return: the temperature in London drops from 46°F to 26°F .

10 Friday

Children aged between 6-11 in Limassol and Famagusta, **Cyprus,** tear down Union Jacks, smash portraits of the royal family, stone British troops and smash car windscreens.
■ The New China News agency announces that a new 30-letter **Latin alphabet** has been given official approval. It will replace around 30,000 ideographic characters used at present. There will be no 'V', but there'll be additional letters for a soft 'G' sound, 'ZH', 'CH', 'SH' and 'NG'.
■ Marshall of the Air Force **Lord Trenchard** (83) dies. He was regarded as the chief architect of British air power.

11 Saturday
New Moon

■ There's the biggest entry ever at **Crufts** Dog Show, Earls Court, London – the cocker spaniel class is largest with 369 dogs entered. The Supreme Champion is a greyhound: *Treetops Golden Falcon*.
RUGBY: England beat Ireland 20-0 in the international at Twickenham . . .

12 Sunday

General Franco drastically curbs civil liberties in Spain following outbreaks of unrest amongst students, who oppose compulsory affiliation to the Falangist student union. Any Spaniard may be banished to any part of the peninsula or any island, be arrested without a warrant and be detained for longer than 72 hrs.
■ More than 600 acres of forest in Glamorgan are destroyed by **fire**. It takes firemen 4hrs to bring the fire under control.

DATELINE: January 11 Notorious British spies Guy Burgess and Donald Maclean, who have been missing since May, 1951, appear in Moscow, and give a press conference. They deny they have ever been Soviet agents.

13 Monday

The **Musicians Union** withdraws all its members from BBC TV programmes because of a dispute over fees.
■ The **great freeze** continues: the Danube is frozen for over 100 miles of its length. Ice-breakers are keeping a shipping channel open on the River Rhine. The US Air Force is flying food, medicine and clothing to Italy, to help people stricken by the worst winter this century.
■ **Cadbury's** reduce the price of milk chocolate by 6d. per lb, as the price of cocoa beans has fallen, and J S Fry & Sons are increasing the weight of their chocolate bars sold for 2d, 3d, 4d, and 6d.

14 Tuesday
St Valentine's Day

Britain's first privately-owned nuclear reactor is to be built at Aldermaston, Berks. Known as **MERLIN** – Medium energy light-water-moderated industrial research reactor – it will be used for research and training by universities.
■ More than 8,000 workers in London printing offices face **dismissal** tomorrow night unless they abandon restrictions on output and overtime ordered by their unions.
. . . More snow: over 12ins falls around Whitby, Yorks, in 24hrs . . .

15 Wednesday

After 9hrs of play, **Chelsea** finally beat Burnley 2-0, at the fifth attempt. They now meet Everton in the fifth round of the FA Cup.

■ The Australian dock strike ends. 20,000 watersiders start work today: 3,500 seamen will begin tomorrow.

■ Heavy **snowfalls** in Yorkshire with drifts up to 16ft.

■ Mrs Iva Toguri d'Aquino – **Tokyo Rose** *(right)* who was imprisoned for broadcasting Japanese propaganda to US troops in World War II, is released after serving 6yrs of her 10yr sentence. She's a native of Los Angeles, a graduate of the University of California, and is married to a Portuguese journalist living in Japan.

16 Thursday

A blitzed site in Upper Thames St, London, is leased to The Mermaid Theatre Trustees to build a **new theatre** – the first to be built in the City of London for nearly 300yrs.

■ Parliament votes to end the **death penalty** by a majority of 31. The Government says it will consider the matter and respond without undue delay.

. . . The BANK RATE is INCREASED by 1% from 4½ % to 5½ %, the highest level since 1932, to control inflation . . .

17 Friday

Chancellor **Harold Macmillan** announces that HP deposits are to rise to 20% (from 15%) on domestic furniture, carpets, cookers and mattresses as a further measure to counter inflation. There will be a £38 million cut in bread and milk subsidies.

■ **Newspaper rationing** is to continue, says Peter Thorneycroft, President of the Board of Trade, though '*The Times* can have more paper because it uses a different kind.'

■ **The Queen** and the Duke of Edinburgh return to London at the end of their Nigerian tour. The temperature in Lagos was 99°F, in London it's 35°F.

18 Saturday

A York aircraft of Scottish Airlines, with 45 servicemen and five crew on board, crashes in Malta. There are no survivors.

■ The USA lifts its **embargo** on shipping arms to the Middle East as suddenly as it was imposed 48hrs ago. 18 American light tanks are being sent to Saudi Arabia, in spite of Jewish protests.

19 Sunday

Over 4 million **olive trees** have been killed by the cold weather in the South of France. It will take 10yrs for the groves to recover to the level of last season's production. Meanwhile, in the continuing **severe weather** in Italy, a postman at Mandella in the Abruzzi is attacked and eaten by wolves.

■ America will make surplus food available for the **relief** of people in distress from the cold weather in Europe.

■ More than 1,500 people flee their homes to escape **floods** in New South Wales, Australia. There is 9ft of water in the streets of South Grafton, when the River Clarence overflows its banks.

20 Monday

A vote of no confidence in members of the parish council is passed (55-2), at a meeting at Moreton-in-the-Marsh, Oxon, after they try to sell their half of the local **duckpond** to the private owner of the other half. The private owner of the half-pond wants to sell it to someone else who would like to clean it up and put the ducks back

■ **Vegetables** are in short supply as crops can't be picked in the ice and snow. Cornwall has its heaviest snowfall of the winter: up to 10ins in the Lizard and Newquay areas. In Kent, snowploughs work 24hrs a day to keep major roads open.

21 Tuesday

The BBC and the Musicians Union reach an **agreement.** Programmes return to normal.

■ The **Duke of Edinburgh's Award** scheme is launched. It is open to boys aged 15-18, and is part of the memorial to the late King George VI.
■ Mr Karamanlis claims victory in the Greek general election.
The Greek Foreign Ministry is unenthusiastic about the latest British proposals for solving the problems in Cyprus.

22 Wednesday

The Rev G P Shelley, minister of Wheatley Park Baptist Church, Doncaster, who was asked to resign when he took a job as a shop assistant to make ends meet, has a new job, as minister of Bromyard Congregational Church in Herefordshire.
■ The Turkish Red Crescent appeals to the Red Cross Societies for extra aid for the 7,000 made homeless by an **earthquake** two days ago at Eskisehir.

23 Thursday

The Calf of Man Crucifixion, one of the earliest **stone carvings** in the British Isles, has been bought by the National Art Collection Fund for £750, and presented to the Manx Museum. It probably dates from the early 7th century.
■ Radio-linked phone calls between Britain, Canada and America have been almost impossible all day because cosmic ray intensity caused a major radio fade-out.

24 Friday

At the 20th congress of Soviet Communist Party, **Nikita Khruschev**, Secretary of the Communist Party of the USSR, denounces Stalin for his pre-war purges, his secret plots to murder critics and friends, and calls into question his military decisions.
■ Two prisoners, who **escaped** from Dover prison early today, are found hiding under the floorboards of a shed in the grounds. Police and dogs have searched for them in snow-covered country for 12hrs.

25 Saturday

The France v England rugby International is postponed, because of bad weather. At Lansdowne Road, Dublin, Ireland beat Scotland 14-10.
■ **Dawn Fraser,** 18 (*left*), of Australia, breaks two world swimming records in a day. She knocks 1.1sec off the previous record for the Women's 200 yds free-style, in a time of 2 min 20.6 sec, and then takes 1.4 secs off the 220 yds freestyle record.
■ 536 men at the Port Talbot steel works strike because management refuses to provide donkey jackets for outside work.

26 Sunday
Full Moon

The chief public **executioner,** Albert Pierrepoint, resigns. In private life he is landlord of a pub near Preston, Lancs.
■ The world record for milk production is claimed for *Clanville Lady Butterfly VIII*, a Dairy Shorthorn from Newstead Grange nr Nottingham. She produced 4,021 gallons in 555 days.
■ Four searchlights, bright enough to be seen in Boston and Baltimore, and 300 miles out in the Atlantic, are being mounted on the 90th storey of the **Empire State Building**, New York, to serve as welcome beacons to visitors each night. Each light costs $250,000, and weighs 1 ton.
... The bread subsidy is cut – the price of a loaf in the UK rises from 7 ½d to 8 ½ d ...

27 Monday

Cuppa woe: The price of refreshments at railway stations goes up by a penny today – a cup of tea will be 5d. and coffee 7d.

■ South African Prime Minister Strydom announces that **Coloured voters** are to be placed on a separate electoral roll.

■ Following 48hrs of storms and heavy rain, a **landslide** carries the engine of an express train into the sea at Ortona, Italy. The rest of the train stays on the rails. The driver and fireman are able to wade ashore.

28 Tuesday

Dolls' houses on show at the **Nuremberg Toy Fair** have miniature electric stoves, fridges, vacuum cleaners, washing machines and TVs. There's also a tractor that works by remote control to a distance of 600ft.

■ A Swiss private collector claims to have purchased a 3ft-high bronze bust of Atropos by Michelangelo in Britain. An Italian expert thinks it is genuine.

29 Wednesday

1,000 workers, the entire force of Mulliners car body builders in Birmingham, are given a week's notice. They have been making bodies for Standard and Triumph.

■ A clause providing for compulsory **safety tests** (see January 26) for cars over 10yrs old at approved garages is added to the Road Traffic Bill. Roadworthy cars will get a test certificate. Uncertified cars will be liable to a £20 fine: further offences will cost £50 or 3 months imprisonment.

■ **President Eisenhower** announces that he will stand for re-election this autumn, but doesn't say whether **Richard Nixon** will be his running mate.

MARCH

1 Thursday
St David's Day

Autherine Lucy (26, *left*) is expelled from Alabama University for 'making unproved charges against the authorities'. The decision is anounced a few hours after the court in Birmingham, Alabama, USA ordered the university to reverse her suspension. Miss Lucy alleges that the university had fostered the riots.

■ Mrs Eliza Sale (88), of Hove, Sussex, who died in January, leaves £40,000 to the **Duke of Argyll**, as she was so proud of belonging to the clan. They had never met.

■ Harold Watkinson, Minister of Transport, says owners will have to pay for the **safety test** on cars. The test will probably cost 5s. or 7s.6d, but it will be some time before testing becomes compulsory.

MARCHING ORDERS F

DATELINE: March 2
King Hussein of Jordan *(right)*, **expels Lieut Gen John Bagot Glubb (Glubb Pasha,** *centre***), the British commander of the Arab Legion and gives him 2hrs to leave the country. It's thought that the King's mother Queen Zein,** *(far right)* **much influenced by a Saudi Arabian envoy, is behind the sacking. Saudi Arabia would like to see the British pull out of the Middle East.**

2 Friday

King Hussein of Jordan expels **Lieut Gen John Bagot Glubb** (Glubb Pasha), the British commander of the Arab Legion (see panel, facing page).

. . . France recognises the independence of Morocco, with the Sultan as the sovereign ruler . . .

3 Saturday

BBC Director General **Sir Ian Jacob** tells the Musicians Union he is still not willing to meet their pay demands, which would cost an estimated £500,000 a year.

■ Two Football Specials taking **Everton** supporters home to Liverpool from Manchester are wrecked after Everton are beaten 2-1 by Manchester City in a sixth-round FA Cup tie.

4 Sunday

Swimmers take advantage of a sunny day at Brighton. Thousands of people head for the South Coast, causing extensive **traffic jams**.

■ Because of the slump in car sales, the credit squeeze and hire purchase restrictions, Standard Motors in Coventry suggests putting 1,250 men on to a 4-day week, with 4 days' pay, but the Joint Shop Stewards' Committee calls for a 36hr week with no pay cuts.

■ The Football Players Union bans floodlit matches, and games on TV, until additional fees are agreed.

RITISH COMMANDER

5 Monday

General Sir John Glubb (Glubb Pasha) is made a KCB. 15 officers attached to Jordan's Arab Legion are recalled: other officers are asked to continue their duties for the time being.

■ Following the failure of peace talks in **Cyprus**, the Royal Corps of Signals jams broadcasts from Athens. The broadcasts are thought to incite terrorists to murder.

■ **Ford** give 40,000 workers a pay rise – 4d. an hour for skilled and semi-skilled workers, 3d. for unskilled workers and women. Sales are going up, and they haven't had to introduce short-time working.

6 Tuesday

Princess Margaret, *above*, is elected President of Britain's newest university – the University College of North Staffordshire, at Keele, Newcastle-under-Lyme. It opened in 1951.

■ Athens decides to discontinue relaying the daily BBC programmes to Greece.

■ 20,000 workers are estimated to be on **short time** in the car industry in Birmingham and Coventry.

■ The North Eastern Gas Board is **prosecuted** by the Ministry of Fuel and fined £10 with 7gns costs for failing to keep up the correct gas pressure in their area.

7 Wednesday

Burton-on-Trent, which suffered a severe **polio epidemic** 4yrs ago, is to boycott a government scheme to vaccinate children. They say there's no guarantee the vaccine will work and there's only enough for one child in five to have it.

■ Heads of government from Egypt, Saudi Arabia and Jordan meet in Cairo and agree to offer **Jordan** a subsidy equalling the £12,000,000 a year paid by Britain.

8 Thursday

Following the **Burgess and Maclean** scandal, the Civil Service orders a crack-down on **security**. Heads of departments must check on employees' private lives and that of their wives. They should watch out for drunkenness, drug addiction, homosexuality, or anything that may affect an official's reliability.

■ **Stan Kenton**, *below*, America's King of Progressive Jazz, has brought his band to Britain by special permission of the Musician's Union. It's the first jazz band to visit for 21yrs. In exchange, Ted Heath and his band are touring America.

SUPER-SONIC!

DATELINE: April 10.

BRITISH pilot Lionel Peter Twiss (34), flying a Fairey Delta 2 research aircraft, sets a new world air-speed record – the first over 1,000 mph – of 1,132 mph in 2 runs over a 9-mile course between Chichester and Ford naval station in Sussex. Twiss's speed is over 300mph faster than the previous record.

9 Friday

Archbishop Makarios and the leaders of the ENOSIS movement in Cyprus are arrested in Nicosia and deported to the Seychelles. The governor says Makarios bought arms for EOKA terrorists, and financed them by taxing Greek Cypriots who wanted baptisms, marriages or funerals.

■ **The Derby** won't be televised this year, as the fees offered by BBC and ITV aren't high enough.

■ Customs officers in Sydney, Australia, remove photos, films and literature from **Sir Eugene Goossens**' luggage and question him for 7hrs. No charges are made. Sir Eugene is conductor of the Sydney Symphony Orchestra.

■ **Ian Macleod**, Minister of Labour, will appoint a committee to investigate the 6-month-old **strike** at the Cammell Laird shipyard where 500 joiners have stopped work because they can't agree with the metal workers about who should drill holes in timber and metal panels on ships.

10 Saturday

Mothering Sunday tomorrow – and the price of some flowers has just gone down, after a fortnight of price rises. **Daffodils** are 3s.6d. to 7s.6d. a dozen. Last year they were 4s.6d.to 8s.6d. a dozen.

11 Sunday

The ban on football under floodlights or on TV is lifted two days before it is due to come into effect.

■ Rioters storm the British Consulate at Heraklion, Crete, protesting at the arrest of **Archbishop Makarios**. The consul escapes by the back door. Troops and police keep 5,000 rioting students away from the British Embassy in Athens.

12 Monday

New Moon

MP Sidney Silverman's bill to abolish **hanging** gets a second reading in the House of Commons. The vote is 286-262 for abolition.

■ Leslie Green, a nurseryman from Bishop's Waltham, Hants, says **Peter Twiss**'s record-breaking flight smashed the glass in a 100ft greenhouse he'd just finished reglazing. As the Ministry of Supply only offered him half of his earlier claim for aircraft damage, he's thinking of suing Twiss and Fairey Aviation.

■ Car dealers rush to Austin Motor Works in Birmingham to collect cars before the price of all **BMC cars** rises at midnight. Cars bought before the deadline can be sold at the old price.

13 Tuesday

The US ambassador in Athens visits the Greek Foreign Minister to express sympathetic concern over recent events in **Cyprus**. The British government is not told of the visit, and a furious Prime Minister **Anthony Eden** orders the ambassador in

WANTED!

DATELINE: APRIL 11 Following a tip-off, 30 policemen and four dogs check 200 caravan dwellers on 2 sites in Chertsey, Surrey, looking for ALFRED HINDS (38), on the run from Nottingham prison. Hinds escaped in November 1955. He was being held for his part in a £35,000 robbery at Maples furniture store. He has conducted an intensive campaign from his prison cell stating his innocence and demanding a new trial.

Washington to demand an explanation.

■ Children at a school in Cricklade, Wilts, have to climb out of a classroom window to go to the lavatory, as the only way out of their classroom is through another class. Managers had asked for a door to be built but got a 5ft high concrete platform with steps and a guard rail outside, and a steep wooden step-ladder inside. The 400yr-old school is an ancient monument, and can't be altered.

■ Players in this year's Cup Final at Wembley will get extra pay for appearing on TV, and a percentage of the total fee paid will go to Players Union benevolent funds.

14 Wednesday

New items on the revised **cost of living** index include TV sets, nylons, washing machines, cars and dog biscuits. 80 new items have been added to the Index of Retail Prices.

■ From Monday, **dockers** will get 2s. a day more, making a basic rate of 28s. a day. They'll also get 1s.6d. in the £ increase on piece work.

15 Thursday

Georgi Malenkov (*right*) minister for electric power in the Soviet government, arrives in Britain for a 3-week visit. His 'study tour', includes a visit to the

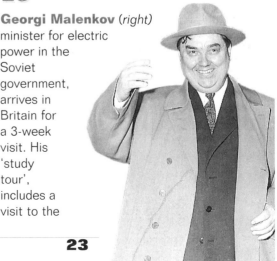

MAR 24

IT is the greatest upset in Grand National history. The Queen Mother's horse, the well-fancied DEVON LOCH, ridden by leading jockey Dick Francis, looks a certain winner of the big Aintree prize, only to mysteriously collapse within sight of the winning post. The race is eventually won by ESB, ridden by Dave Dick.

DEVON LOCH STUMBLES WIT

House of Commons and Stratford. He will also be shown round Canterbury Cathedral by the 'Red Dean', Dr Hewlett Johnson, and go to the Grand National at Aintree.

■ **My Fair Lady,** starring Rex Harrison and Julie Andrews, opens on Broadway to rapturous reviews.

■ All 600 lines to the London weather forecast (dial WEA 2211) have been in use for the first time, say the Post Office. People were worried by darkness at 4.00 pm, caused by a layer of thick smoke trapped over the city by heavy cloud.

16 Friday

Twelve people booked on the sleeper for Glasgow find that the 2 sleeping cars aren't attached to the train when it arrives at Euston. They have to wait for a 'special', with an engine and the two sleepers, to be made up: it leaves London 2½ hrs late.

. . . A severe earthquake in southern Lebanon. More than 130 people die, 500 are injured, and 10,000 made homeless . . .

17 Saturday

St Patrick's Day

Talks between employers and the two unions involved in the printing dispute break down after 9hrs. Over 15,000 men are idle.

■ **Postmen** are to get electric trucks like milk floats for delivering mail in districts where it will be economical.

18 Sunday

Six MPs are told to 'nip out' when an independence rally in **Singapore** turns into a riot. The crowd breaks through a police cordon at Kallang Airport and pelts the airport building with bricks and bottles.

■ The President of the Pedestrians' Association for Road Safety says that **women drivers** are safest. In 45,000 out of 60,000 cases, the pedestrian victims of accidents are said to be 'heedless of traffic'.

19 Monday

Three ambulances are waiting at the quay in Southampton to take the badly injured to hospital when the *Queen Mary* docks after 3 days of 70mph winds on the 5-day Atlantic crossing. More than 100 people are hurt, about 7,000 pieces of crockery are smashed, and dozens of deckchairs lost.

■ The railways are given 6 months to put forward drastic new plans to increase

National Glory in Sight

efficiency and cut losses, or fares will rise.

■ The heat from a **blazing lorry** at Patchway, nr Bristol, is so intense the eggs in the crates on another lorry standing nearby are cooked.

20 Tuesday

The Royal Commission on Marriage and Divorce recommends three new grounds for **divorce**, including wilful refusal to consummate a marriage. The 400-page report shows the 19 members disagreed completely on every major proposal for divorce law changes.

■ Viewers will see more stars on their screens following the settlement between the BBC and the Musicians Union. It will allow the BBC to pre-record TV shows with music, featuring stars when they're available.

■ Tunisia becomes independent, under President **Habib Bourguiba**. It's been a French dependency since 1881.

21 Wednesday

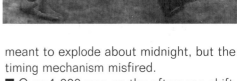

The Governor of Cyprus, Sir John Harding, sleeps on a **time bomb** for 8hrs! It was hidden between two mattresses, and was meant to explode about midnight, but the timing mechanism misfired.

■ Over 1,000 men on the afternoon shift at Workington Steel Works are sent home, because there is no fuel oil for the blast furnaces. 18 oil tankers, carrying 300 tons of oil, have been lost by British Rail on the 80-mile rail journey from Heysham to Workington. Spotter planes find the tankers just outside Heysham.

22 Thursday

Employers reject a claim by 5 unions for **equal pay for women** in general engineering. This would have increased pay by £1.17s.10d. per week for 200,000 women.

■ Colonel General Serov, the head of the Russian Secret Police, known in the West as '**Ivan the Terrible**', arrives in London to prepare for the visit of Bulganin and Khruschev in April, in a civilian version of the secret twin-jet bomber, the TU 104, designed by A Tupolev and known as 'The Badger'.

... Greek Cypriot servants are banned from the homes of Sir John Harding and other British officials serving in Cyprus ...

LIGHT BLUES COME HOME IN STYLE

DATELINE: March 24: In the Boat Race, Cambridge beat Oxford by 1¼ lengths in 18min 36sec. It's the fourth fastest time in the history of the race from Putney to Mortlake.

23 Friday

The Queen lays the foundation stone of the new **Coventry Cathedral**, designed by Basil Spence. The old cathedral was destroyed by bombing on November 24, 1940.

■ **Pakistan** becomes an **independent** Islamic Republic within the Commonwealth.

24 Saturday

The *Theron* arrives back at Tower Bridge after a 4-month trip to the Weddell Sea in Antarctica.

.. Grand National sensation as Devon Loch falls with victory in sight [See pages 24-25] ...

25 Sunday

Palm Sunday

Robert Newton (51, *below)*, the British character actor, dies. He's known to millions of children for his portrayal of Long John Silver and his 'Aaah Jim Lad'.

■ After a week-long **strike**, the times of the afternoon shift at Wharncliffe Woodmoor Colliery, Barnsley, Yorks, have been changed so that the miners can get home in time to see TV.

... General elections in Tunisia – Habib Bourguiba forms a government ...

26 Monday

Full Moon

Mrs Audrey Critchley meets three Mau Mau terrorists on a lonely road outside Nairobi, Kenya, and persuades them to surrender. She then drives them to the nearest police station, in Gilgil.

■ Boys from Heriot's School, Edinburgh, are blamed for placing a newspaper-wrapped bomb on tram tracks in the city. It blows in a tram's windows, makes a hole in the floor, and the clippie is knocked down by the blast.

The 20 passengers aboard are unhurt.
■ The Bishop of Birmingham is attacked by Congregationalists for attending a brewers' dinner and drinking a glass of wine. They say his presence at the dinner was shameful.

27 Tuesday

The shut-down of **Ally Pally** – millions of viewers watch as Britain's No 1 TV station Alexandra Palace *(right)* shuts down. From tomorrow, BBC programmes for the south will come from the new £500,000 Crystal Palace transmitter.

28 Wednesday

Some viewers get a dazzling white screen and no picture as a result of yesterday's transmitter changes. TV sets are getting a much stronger signal than usual.
■ The Playhouse, Derby, is almost totally destroyed by a **fire**, which starts near the stage and sweeps through the auditorium: the roof collapses.
■ The great 3-day **fog** in January killed nearly 1,000 people in Greater London.

29 Thursday
Maundy Thursday

Prince Alfonso of Bourbon (14), the younger son of **Don Juan**, pretender to the Spanish throne, is accidentally killed when cleaning a pistol at his home in Estoril, Portugal.
■ **Apartheid** is introduced in offices and amenities under municipal control in Cape Town, South Africa.
■ A 3ins mortar shell is found under a road bridge across the River Tawe nr Swansea Docks. Police think boys found it and carried it to the bridge. Sappers take the shell away to make it safe.
. . . THE QUEEN distributes Maundy money to 30 men and 30 women [the recipients match the Queen's age, and she'll be 30 on April 21] . . .

30 Friday
Good Friday

Two British battalions and support troops (about 2,200 fighting men) will be withdrawn from **Kenya** by June. There will be a general election in Kenya in September, which will include black voters for the first time.
■ At the British **Marbles** Championship at Tinsley Green, Sussex, *(pictured below)* a crowd of about 1,000 see the Tinsley Green Tigers, champions for the past 5yrs, beaten. Toolmaker Billy Wright wins the individual title for the third time. He has a hot water bottle under his coat to keep his fingers warm. England beat Wales in the International match.

31 Saturday

A battalion of Grenadier Guards, the last combatant British troops in the **Suez** Canal Zone, sail for home, after 74yrs of British presence in Egypt. The last RAF base will be evacuated by 14 April.
. . . The Queen's horse, HIGH VELDT, wins the 2,000 Guineas trial stakes at Kempton Pk. . .
■ General Kenryo Sato, former head of Japan's Military Affairs bureau, is released from Sugamo

THE FASHION HIGHSPOT

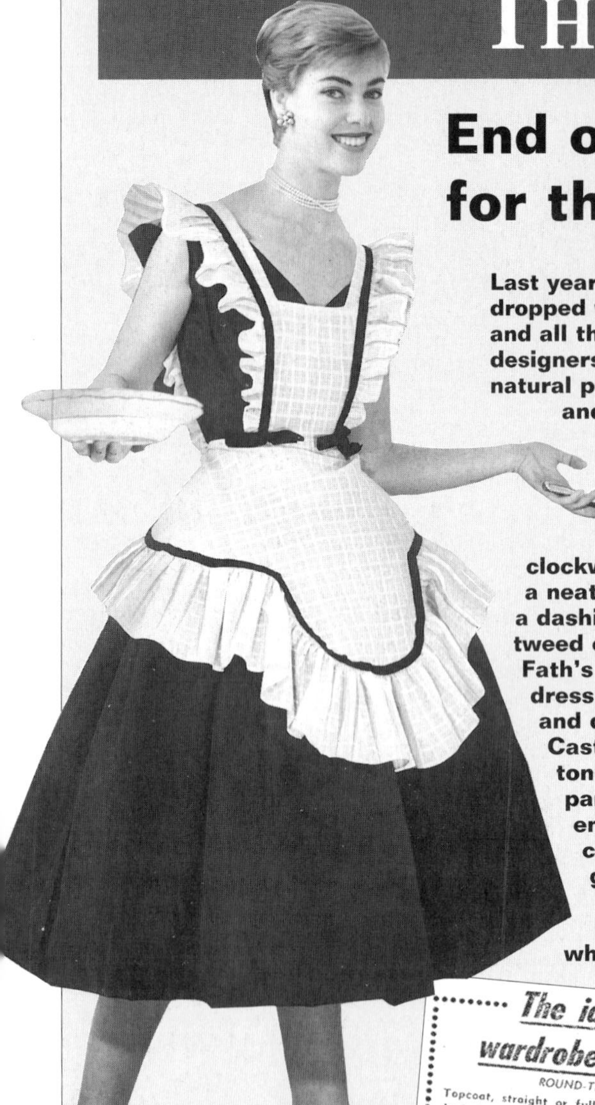

End of the line for the A line

Last year's A line, with its dropped waistline is no more, and all the major Paris designers restore the waist to its natural position. Hats are small, and coats are big. Trousers are tapered to the ankle, and worn with flat pumps and chunky-knit sweaters. Pictured clockwise from right, a neatly waisted summer suit; a dashing black-and-white tweed cape by Dior; Jacques Fath's chiffon afternoon dress; a sophisticated cape and dress from Lanvin Castillo; a crop-waisted cotton top worn with tapered pants; a dashing Italian ensemble; a practical chunky knit; winter elegance from Paris; a dressy apron to cover your evening dress while you fix supper.

The ideal basic wardrobe – for £100!

The ideal basic wardrobe—for £100

ROUND-THE-YEAR WEAR	£	s
Topcoat, straight or full	8	0
Jacket	3	10
Suit, classic or semi-classic in basic shade ...	8	0
Cocktail dress or set of party separates ...	6	10
Two skirts (one full or pleated, one slim) ...	5	0
Two day dresses	8	10
Raincoat in poplin, doubling as summer coat	5	0
Two cotton shirts	2	10
Two sweaters (or one sweater and one cardigan buttoning to neck)	3	0
Stole (wool or fur fabric)	1	10
Two handbags (one daytime, one cocktail)	3	10
Three pairs gloves	1	10
Two hats	2	10
Three pairs shoes (one suede, one leather, one evening style)	8	0
Underwear and stockings (including a stiff petticoat)	7	0
Artificial jewellery, scarves, etc.	2	0
HOLIDAY WEAR		
Two cotton dresses (or one dress and one set of separates)...	7	0
Two swimsuits	4	0
Pair of shorts and pair of jeans	2	0
Beach jacket	1	10
Strapless sun-top	1	0
Summer handbag	1	10
Two pairs of shoes (including sandals) ...	4	0
Beach accessories (including bag, towel, cap, etc.)	3	0
TOTAL ...	£100	0

OF 1956

Gaol, Tokyo. He was condemned to life imprisonment in 1948 as a **war criminal**, and is the last of 28 Class A war criminals to be freed on parole after the completion of 10yrs.

APRIL

1 Sunday
Easter Day

The **Louvre** is shut, preventing tens of thousands of holiday-makers in Paris for Easter from visiting. Museum attendants are on strike.

■ The first US **U-2 spy planes** arrive in Britain and touch down at Lakenheath where they will be based.

■ From today until October 15 pilots are forbidden to fly lower than 2,000 ft over Caps Wood Buffalo Park in Canada's N W Territories, or land in the protected area, so that nesting whooping cranes won't be disturbed.

. . . London has the coldest Easter weekend for 5yrs. The west of Britain has 10hrs sunshine – after early frost the temperature rises to 53° F . . .

2 Monday

Japan didn't have a white Christmas, but it has a **white Easter**. The traditional cherry-blossom viewing in Tokyo and other cities is stopped by freak weather as rain turns to snow in winds from Siberia. The temperature drops to 39°F.

■ Egyptians are being offered free '**ride a MiG**' trips, so they learn to appreciate the Soviet armaments of their armed forces. All hopeful passengers are told to get a medical to see that their hearts are OK, and not to have breakfast.

1956 PRICE LIST

TV Licence	**£3.00**
Radio Licence	**£2.00**
Income tax (standard)	**8s.6d. in the £**
Dog licence	**7s.6d.**
Birth certificate	**3s.9d.**
Marriage certificate	**3s.9d.**
Death certificate	**3s.9d.**
Stamp (inland)	**2½d.**
(overseas)	**4d.**
Family Allowance (1st 2 children 10s for third and subsequent)	**8s. wk**
Old Age Pension	**2s.-26s. per wk**

3 Tuesday

The BBC give a demonstration of **colour television** transmission at Alexandra Palace.

■ The Cunard liner *Franconia* arrives back safely in Southampton. The port turbine broke down 450 miles out from Le Havre and it had to abandon its voyage to Halifax, Nova Scotia.

■ **Fires** caused when moor burning got out of hand over Easter destroyed nearly 900 acres of Forestry Commission plantation in Scotland.

■ **Tornadoes** in 8 American states claim 40 lives, injuring at least 22, and causing an estimated $15,000,000 damage. Valentine, Nebraska, has 2½ feet of snow, and is completely cut off except by radio, when 70mph winds and heavy icing bring down power lines.

4 Wednesday

The chairman of the Olympic Games Committee in **Melbourne**, where the games will be held in November, is calling for tenders as the Committee objects to TV companies worldwide using pressure tactics to try and get film rights for the games for little or nothing.

■ The Australian Immigration Department says that genuine tourists from the Soviet Union will be allowed to visit for the Olympic Games – but the ban on other Iron Curtain visitors will remain.

■ Troops using **mine-detectors** find 53 sticks of dynamite in a walled-up safe at Kykko Monastery nr Nicosia, Cyprus. The monks say they didn't know the safe existed.

5 Thursday

The *Perseverance*, an 84yr-old stage coach which used to run between Leatherhead and Box Hill,

WHAT'S ON AT THE THEATRE

THE big West End hits of the year are The Quare Fellow (left), the Brendan Behan play starring Maxwell Shaw and Gerry Raffles; and John Osborne's Look Back in Anger, (right), with Kenneth Haigh, Alan Bates (seated) and Mary Ure.

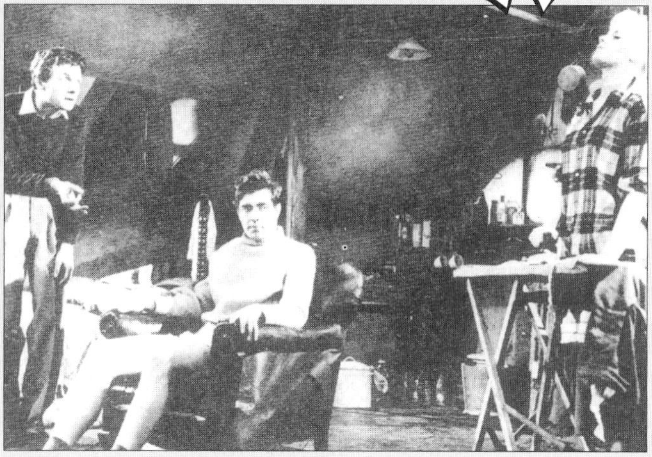

THE PYJAMA GAME	Edmund Hockridge, Max Wall, Joy Nichols, Elizabeth Seal
THE QUARE FELLOW	by Brendan Behan, with Maxwell Shaw, Gerry Raffles.
WALTZ OF THE TOREADORS	by Jean Anouilh, with Hugh Griffiths, Walter Hudd, Beatrix Lehmann, Brenda Bruce
THE CHALK GARDEN	by Edith Bagnold, with Felix Aylmer, Dame Edith Evans, Peggy Ashcroft
SOUTH SEA BUBBLE	by Noel Coward, with Arthur Macrae, Ian Hunter, Ronald Lewis, Vivian Leigh
GIGI	by Colette and Anita Loos, with Tony Britton, Esme Percy, Leslie Caron
UNDER MILK WOOD	by Dylan Thomas, with William Squire, Donald Houston, Aubrey Richards
ROMANOFF AND JULIET	by Peter Ustinov, with Peter Ustinov, Freerick Valp, Edward Atienza, Katy Vail
LOOK BACK IN ANGER	by John Osborne, with Kenneth Haigh, Alan Bates, Helena Hughes, Mary Ure
THE THREEPENNY OPERA	by Bertold Brecht and Kurt Weil, with Bill Owen, Eric Pohlmann, Lisa Lee

Surrey, leaves the Festival Hall, London on its 24-town tour for the Roads Campaign Council, publicising their demand for a 10yr, £75million programme to develop a modern road system in Britain.

■ Fighting breaks out in the **Gaza Strip**. Egypt shells three Israeli settlements: The Israelis reply with artillery, shelling Gaza town for 2hrs.

6 Friday

Floral Hall, part of **Covent Garden** Market, is badly damaged by fire. The adjoining Royal Opera House is unscathed.

■ A Spanish **donkey** leaves Paris by air for Washington. It's a goodwill present from Spain's General Franco to **President Eisenhower,** wishing him luck in the forthcoming election. The donkey is a Republican party symbol.

■ The 6,000 employees of the Rootes Group in Coventry are back to full-time working. At Dagenham, the production of **Ford Popular** cars is cut from 145 to 120 a day, and 200 Ford workers are given notice.

7 Saturday

Wladislaw Gomulka, former Secretary of the Polish Communist Party and Deputy Premier, who was imprisoned without trial in 1950 accused of deviationism and 'Titoism' for advocating a Polish way to socialism, is released from prison.

. . . OXFORD beats Cambridge 87-39 at the University Sports Match at the White City – Oxford's ninth win in succession . . .

■ 2,000 men employed at Cambrian collieries, Clydach Vale, Rhondda, who have been on unofficial **strike** for 11 days over piece-workers' rates, and the men from

6 other Rhondda pits who have come out in sympathy, will return to work on Monday.

8 Sunday

A memorial on the wall of St Bartholomew's Hospital, London, to the Scottish patriot Sir William Wallace, who was executed at Bartholomew's Fair, Smithfield, in 1305, is unveiled by Lady Dundee.

■ **Beer drinking** in Germany has increased – it's now about 120 pints a year per head of population. The average drinker gets through about 200 pints a year.

■ The Knesset gives Israeli Prime Minister **David Ben-Gurion**, who is also Minister of Defence, emergency powers to requisition any equipment he needs, and every male resident of Israel must carry an identity card at all times.

9 Monday

About 150 children in Kilmhurst, S Yorks, are kept away from school because free transport facilities have been withdrawn.

■ Parents refuse to allow their children to walk or cycle nearly 3 miles to Haugh Road Secondary Modern, Rawmarsh, as the road passes over a railway crossing, is near a canal, is only partly lit and has no footpath at its narrowest part.

■ **Fire** badly damages the central part of Derby High School for Girls. Classrooms have been rifled, and there are other suspicious circumstances. The 300 girls are on holiday, but the headmistress says the new term will start as planned.

10 Tuesday

The London Fire Services **war memorial** 1939-45 is unveiled in the London Fire Brigade HQ by Home Secretary Major Lloyd George, and dedicated by the Archbishop of Canterbury.

■ 200,000 **nurses** will get a pay rise ranging from £20 – £95pa.

■ **Dr Walter Gropius** (72), is presented with the Royal Gold Medal for Architecture, 1956. Dr Gropius is the originator of the Bauhaus idea and was director of the

GRACE KELLY STA

Fairytale Wedding of the Year . . .

FILM STAR GRACE KELLY, a star in *High Society*, joins royal society when she marries PRINCE RAINIER III of Monaco in Monte Carlo on April 19. The fairytale wedding captures the imagination of the world. The bride's wedding dress and veil are made of 25yds of peau de soie, 25yds silk taffeta, 100yds silk net, and 300yds ivory-coloured lace. She carries a small bunch of lilies of the valley, and her bridesmaids are in primrose organdie. There are 1,200 guests, including dignitaries from 25 countries. After the service the happy couple drive through cheering crowds in the the streets of Monte Carlo in an open black-and-yellow car, before leaving for their honeymoon cruise on the prince's yacht *Deo Juvante II*.

. . . But She's Not Alone in the Dash to the Altar!

STAR WEDDINGS OF 1956 (*clockwise from top left*): Actor Anthony Steel and actress Anita Ekberg; Marilyn Monroe and playwright Arthur Miller at their Jewish ceremony; Fiona Campbell-Walter and Baron Heinrich von Thyssen-Bornemisza de Kaszon marry in Lugano, Switzerland; heiress Gloria Vanderbilt and television director Sidney Lumet wed in New York.

Bauhaus, which had enormous influence on architectural theory, from 1919-28. He came to England in 1934, then went on to become Professor of Architecture at Harvard University, USA.

■ Singer **Nat King Cole** is dragged off the stage by a group of white men as he sings to a white audience in Birmingham, Alabama, USA.

11 Wednesday

New Moon

380,000 Civil Service office staff (not main Post Office staff) get a 5-day working week with effect from 1 July.

■ It's the second day of a **strike** at Macy's, New York, the biggest department store in the world. The shop opens at the usual time, though it is surrounded by 2,500 pickets. Supervisors and company officers man the counters.

■ Burton-on-Trent town council decides to accept the polio **vaccination** scheme (see March 7). The only town that hasn't joined the scheme now is Wakefield, Yorks.

for good taste and good times
Let's have a
BABY BUBBLY
the sparkling Champagne Perry
It's gay, it's grand it's obtainable at all bars and licensed houses
BABY BUBBLY
Goldwell
Champagne Perry
BABY BUBBLY 1/3
PER BOTTLE
Obtainable in the Party Size Bottle at 7/6

12 Thursday

Berthe Morisot's painting, *Jour d'Eté*, is stolen from the Tate Gallery. The Irish National Students council admits responsibility for the theft. The picture is part of the Lane bequest, the subject of a dispute between Dublin and London since Sir Hugh Lane, former director of the National Gallery of Ireland, divided his collection between the two cities on his death.

■ The proposed new road crossing for the River Forth, Scotland, will be a **suspension bridge** with a main span of 3,300ft, and suspended side spans of 1,260ft. The estimated cost is £9,960,000.

■ Doncaster, Yorks, is giving old people portable fire **alarms**. They're automatic, and will go off as soon as the temperature reaches danger point.

13 Friday

Several MPs call for the reintroduction of the **groat**, a coin worth 4d, so it can be used in phone boxes when calls go up to 4d. in July. The groat was first coined about 1351, though for the past 200 years or so it's only been used in Maundy money.

■ A standard showing a **Madonna** and 2 saints painted by Raphael is found in the municipal storeroom in the town hall of Gubbio, Umbria, Italy.

14 Saturday

London Zoo will not open late on Saturdays this year. The public response last year was disappointing.

■ A device is demonstrated in Chicago which records TV programmes on **magnetic tape** and plays them back.

. . . FRANCE beat England 14-9 in the Five-Nations'

OVIET LEADERS IN SALUTE TO KARL MARX

BRITAIN rolls out the red carpet for Soviet leaders Nikita Khruschev and Marshal Bulganin. They arrive in Portsmouth on board the 112,800 ton cruiser *Ordjonikidze* **(formerly** *Konigsberg***) for a 10-day visit. They are taken on a 2hr sight-seeing tour of London before taking up residence at Claridges Hotel. First stop is Highgate Cemetary,** *left***, where they place a wreath at the tomb of Communist icon Karl Marx. Talks with the British Government are followed by the signing of a joint communique at Downing Street, with Prime Minister Sir Anthony Eden,** *right.*

rugby championship. WALES win the title, with England, France and Ireland all tying for 2nd place. Scotland gets the wooden spoon.

15 Sunday

General Motors Corporation in America has developed a car that can run on peanut oil, paraffin, or other fuel. Research has been going on for 5yrs, though they can't say when it will become a commercial proposition.

■ The National Union of Small Shopkeepers recommends its 11,000 members to increase **retail prices** by 5% unless the government promises to review the 'vicious' rate reassessments of business premises.

16 Monday

Berthe Morisot's painting, *Jour d'Eté,* which was stolen from the Tate Gallery on April 11, is returned unharmed to the Irish Embassy, in a parcel addressed to the ambassador.

■ English importers are trying to bring in as many **potatoes** as possible before Saturday, when the Dutch have banned their free export. Wholesalers are hopeful that enough potatoes can be imported this week to last until the end of May, when the first new potatoes from Jersey are due.

■ **Apartheid** is to be enforced on Cape Town's buses and trams from today. Downstairs seats will be for Europeans, upstairs for 'all classes'. In Port Elizabeth, whites prefer the cheaper 'all classes' buses to the more expensive 'whites only' ones.

17 Tuesday
Budget Day

In the **Budget**, Harold Macmillan, Chancellor of the Exchequer, introduces a **Premium Bonds** scheme with tax-free prizes of £1,000. Family allowances will go up by 2s. a week to 10s; 2d. goes on the price of 20 cigarettes. The bread subsidy will end – a 1¾ lb loaf will rise by 1½d. The stamp duty on house purchase is reduced.

■ The Italians are to build a new **autostrada** from Milan to Naples. It will be 740km (about 450 miles) long. Work will start by the end of April; it will take 8-9yrs to complete, and cost about £110,000,000.

■ Dr Walter B Emery, of London University, has discovered the 5,000yr-old tomb of 1st Thinite Dynasty Queen **Her Nit** in a dig at Saqqara, nr Cairo, Egypt. The tomb contains a fine cup made of schist and pink limestone, and a necklace of gold and cornelian which is the finest piece of 1st dynasty jewellery discovered to date.

18 Wednesday

Green **vegetables** will be in short supply until June, says the Ministry of Agriculture.

■ Following the murder by EOKA gunmen of a Greek Cypriot policeman who was visiting his wife and baby in hospital, Nicosia starts a week's 'penance'. All restaurants, bars, clubs, coffee shops, cinemas, etc., owned by Greek Cypriots must close for a week.

19 Thursday

Prince Rainier III (32) of Monaco marries film star **Grace Kelly** (26) at St Nicholas' Cathedral in Monte Carlo *(see page 32)*.

■ A **Noah's Ark** aircraft arrives in Dar-es-Salaam on its way to Kerguelen Island in the Indian Ocean. It carries 6 reindeer, rabbits, goats, wild sheep from Corsica, hens, ducks, and a pair of turtle doves. It's hoped they will breed, and help feed the island population.

20 Friday

The **Badminton** 3-day event is won by *Kilbarry*, ridden by Lieut Col F Weldon, captain of the British Olympic equestrian team.

■ The **oldest person** in the Soviet Union, Mazhmud Eivasor, said to be 148, is presented with the Order of the Red Banner of Labour in Baku.

ELVIS PI

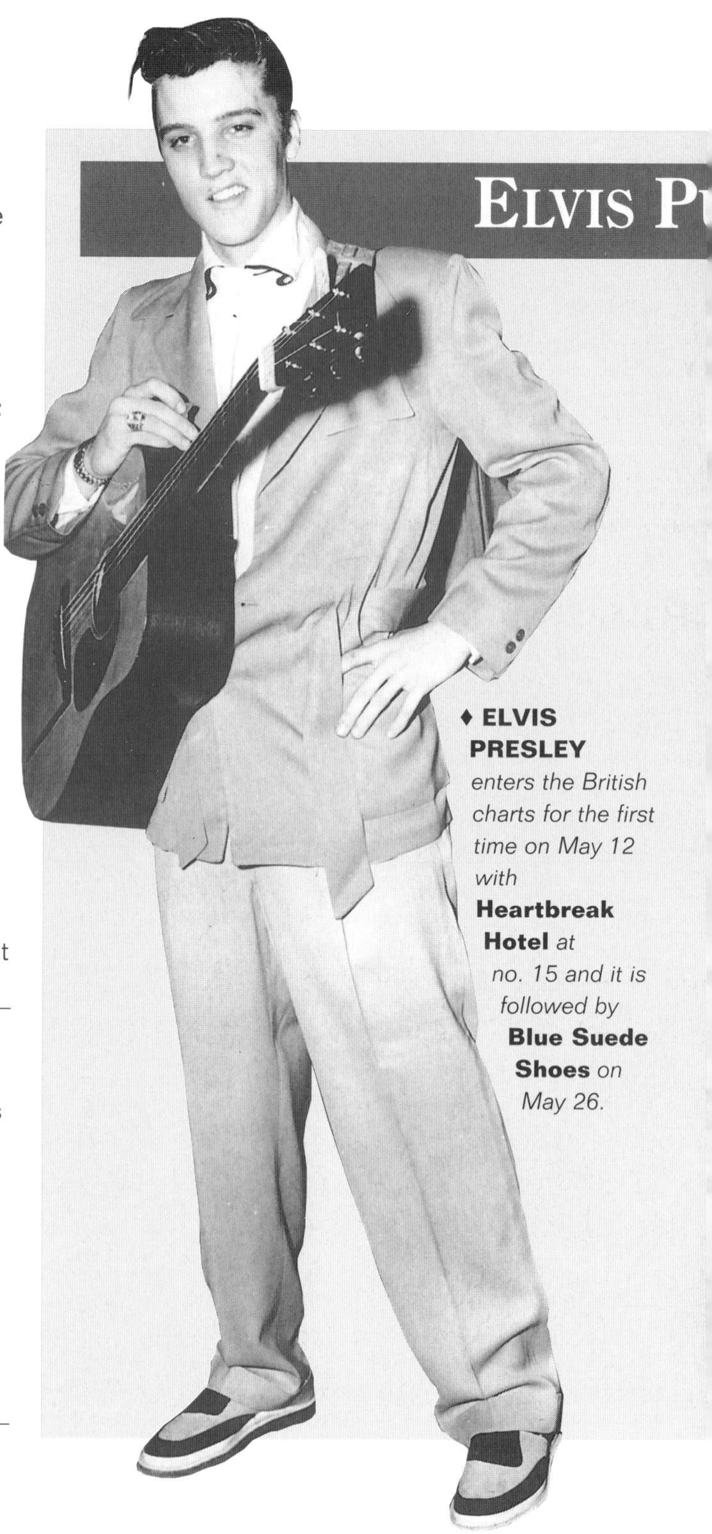

♦ **ELVIS PRESLEY** *enters the British charts for the first time on May 12 with* **Heartbreak Hotel** *at no. 15 and it is followed by* **Blue Suede Shoes** *on May 26.*

21 Saturday

The **Queen's birthday** – she's 30 today. Cossacks ride two horses into the Royal Mews at Buckingham Palace – *Melekush*, for the Duke of Edinburgh, a 3yr-old Azerbaijani, and *Zaman* for Prince Charles,

ON HIS BLUE SUEDE SHOES TO SHAKE UP POP

HART BUSTERS OF '56

t Walkin' in the Rain – Johnnie Ray
' weeks)
Down Your Arms – Anne Shelton
weeks)
Voman in Love – Frankie Lane
weeks)

OP BRITISH SONGS

the Fountains of Rome
eams Can Tell a Lie
y Down Your Arms
September Love
Unfinished Symphony
llie the Elephant
t of Town
kin' the Chicken
ck with the Cavemen
mmer Song
e March Hare
d Pi-anna Rag
u Are My First Love

MOVERS AND SHAKERS

☆ **Lonnie Donegan** is a hit with *Rock Island Home*..**Pat Boone's** *I'll Be Home*, is his biggest-ever UK seller.
☆ **The Goons** *(below, left)* make their first record, *I'm Walking Backwards for Christmas*, which appears at no. 4 in the Charts on July 14. They follow up with the popular and zany *Ying Tong Song*
☆ **Doris Day**'s *Whatever Will Be, Will Be (Que Sera Sera)*, from the film *The Man Who Knew Too Much*, in which she starred with James Stewart, wins the Oscar for best song from a film.
☆ On September 9, **Bill Haley and his Comets** have five entries in the Top 20 – *Rockin' thru the Rye, The Saints Rock, Razzle Dazzle, Rock Around the Clock and See You Later, Alligator.*
☆ On November 10, **Tommy Steele**, *(right)* Britain's first Rock'n'Roller enters the Top Twenty at No 10 with *Rock with the Cavemen*. He achieves even greater success with *Singin' the Blues*.

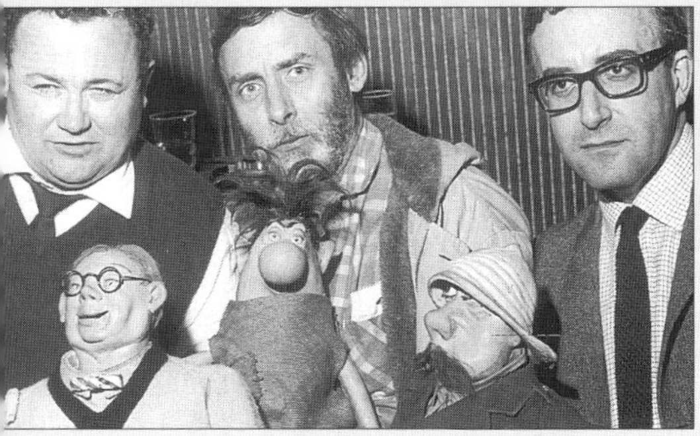

a 4yr-old Turkman. They are both golden, with black manes and tails, and are gifts from Marshal Bulganin and Nikita Khruschev.
■ 150yrs after its construction by Napoleon's engineers, the Simplon Pass is blocked by snow, and a snowplough, called Napoleon, can't break through. An avalanche 27ft deep and 150ft wide has cut off Simplon village on the southern side.

22 Sunday

Khruschev and **Bulganin** meet the Queen at Windsor Castle. They present her with a small bear-cub called Nikki for Princess Anne. The bear will soon be on view at London Zoo.
■ The wreck of the barque *Scottish Prince* which sank in 1887, at Southport,

Sharks Circle Round Crabb Amid Fishy Goings-on in Depths of Portsmouth Harbour!

DATELINE: April 29. **War hero COMMANDER LIONEL CRABB, 46** *(above)* **fails to return from a test dive in Stokes Bay, Portsmouth, and sparks a diplomatic incident. He was reported missing a day after the** *Ordjonikidze* **arrived with Khruschev and Bulganin** *(right)*. **Police tore pages out of the register of the hotel where Crabb had stayed, questions are asked in Parliament and Britain eventually sends a note of apology to Russia. Cdr Crabb was awarded the George Medal in 1944.**

nr Brisbane, Australia, is found by the Queensland Underwater Research Group. Hampered by 3 sharks and a stingray, divers eventually get into the wreck and come out with 5 bottles – 3 Scotch whisky and 2 Irish whiskey – part of the barque's cargo.

■ The Motor and Motorcycle Museum at Beaulieu is opened by **Lord Brabazon** of Tara and Geoff Duke, the world motorcycle racing champion. The museum contains 41 motorcycles and 24 cars, and is the first motorcycle museum in the world.

23 Monday

St George's Day

For the first time ever, the **Jewel Tower** at the Palace of Westminster opens to the

UNBEATEN ROCKY CALLS IT A DAY

public. It's the last surviving part of the mediaeval palace built in 1365-66 by Edward III to house his private jewelry and plate.

■ Stratford-on-Avon, Warks, celebrates **William Shakespeare**'s 392nd birthday. Representatives of 88 countries join in a procession from his birthplace to the church, where flowers are put on his grave.

■ The 13-day strike at **Macy's** department store in New York is over. The main store and 4 suburban branches never closed, as 1,500 senior employees, friends and relatives manned the counters.

24 Tuesday

Newspapers in Moscow report that Khruschev and Bulganin have been presented with Jaguar sports cars by the British government.

■ Sir Henry Cohen, Professor of Medicine at Liverpool, says **cancer** of the lung kills more people than any other disease. Enquiries all over the world show smoking is the cause. There is an 8% chance of lung cancer for a man smoking over 20 cigarettes a day.

25 Wednesday

Full Moon

Dr Michael Ramsay is enthroned as Archbishop of York.

■ Most of the French expeditionary force has left **South Vietnam**. The last 3,000 are clearing up, and should be out by June 3.

■ 1,610,000 children, all born between 1947-1954, are registered for **polio vaccination** in England and Wales. The total number eligible is estimated at 5,542,000.

■ **Rocky Marciano,** 33, *(above)* never defeated as a professional boxer and world heavyweight champion since 1952, has decided to call it a day. He achieved the perfect record of 49 fights, 49 wins, in which only five opponents even survived to hear the bell.

26 Thursday

11,000 production workers at Standard Motor Co, Coventry, go on **strike** because shop stewards haven't been given a chance to discuss short-time working as an alternative to lay-offs in summer.

■ **President Eisenhower** *(left)* says he's delighted that **Richard Nixon** will definitely be seeking re-election as Vice President of the USA – there have been rumours that some Republicans wanted another candidate.

27 Friday

Stanley Matthews, now 42, is back in the England football team to play Brazil in May.

■ Several hundred workers at the Pressed Steel Co car body factory at Cowley, Oxford, are idle because of the Standard workers' strike.

■ Speakers at the congress of the Royal Society of Health say that workers face health problems because of **stress** caused by travelling.

28 Saturday

Ferrari takes the first five places in the Mille Miglia race in Italy. **Peter Collins,** GB, *(right)*, who drives for Ferrari, is second. Driving conditions are appalling, and there are five deaths.

■ A new **radio telescope** comes into operation at Harvard University. Weighing 4 tons, with a diameter of 60ft and mounted on a 50ft tower, it can be focussed on any part of the sky.

29 Sunday

■ The **world population** reached a total of 2,652,000,000 in 1954 – well over half of it in Asia, according to figures published by the UN today. China has the biggest population – 82,000,000. The biggest cities are New York, London, and Tokyo. Women live longer than men in every country. In England and Wales, male life expectancy is 67.3yrs, and female is 72.4yrs.

30 Monday

Bulganin and **Khruschev** are back in Moscow after their visit to Britain. They say their trip was a success, though they criticize the Labour party for attempts 'to spoil the friendly atmosphere'.

■ The **Duke of Edinburgh**, the patron of the Central Council for Physical Recreation, makes a TV broadcast on their 21st anniversary. He says the council wants to encourage people to do something with their leisure.

MAY

1 Tuesday

For the first time, the total number of **wireless sets** in the world (257 million) is greater than the total circulation of all daily newspapers (255 million). The circulation of daily papers has gone up 14% in the last 5 yrs, but ownership of wirelesses has gone up by 41%. There are 44 million TV sets in the world.

■ **Oxford University** votes to confer an honorary law degree on ex-President **Harry S Truman** of the USA.

2 Wednesday

The Minister of Education is asking local education authorities to halve the amount of potatoes served in **school meals**, because of shortages. Substitutes suggested are bread, rice, spaghetti, macaroni, pastry fingers, dumplings and scones.

■ The National Insurance Advisory Committee suggests the amount of money pensioners are allowed to earn before their **pensions** are reduced should be increased from 40s. to 50s. a week.

■ The **King of Nepal**, HM Mahendra Bir Bikram Shah Deva, the only Hindu monarch in the world, and Queen Ratna Rajya Laxmi, are crowned in Katmandu. The Hindu gods and goddesses were formally invited to be present, and a brown cow is brought in to witness the ceremony.

3 Thursday

Protest march by more than 100 seamen in Perth, W. Australia, concerned about the **atomic tests** due to be carried out in the Monte Bello Islands later this month. Their demands include protective clothing for all ships' crews on the coastal run, a pledge that all ships will be kept outside a 500-mile radius of the explosion, and all coastal ships to have Geiger counters.

■ A mass meeting at the Standard Motor Co, Coventry, votes to stay out after management say 'no comment' to their terms for a return to work.

■ A **£10,000 reward** is offered by the Governor of Cyprus for information leading to the arrest of George Theodorus **Grivas**, thought to be Dighenis, the leader of the terrorist movement.

City's Cup hero plays on with broken neck . . .

MANCHESTER CITY's German goalkeeper Bert Trautmann makes another brave save at the feet of a Birmingham forward. He is instrumental in the Manchester club's 3-1 FA Cup Final victory at Wembley, playing for the last 20 minutes with a neck injury following another collision. It is only after the game that doctors find he has broken a bone in his neck. Manchester United have already won the League Championship – the last time both big prizes went to one city was in 1906 when Everton won the Cup and Liverpool the League.

4 Friday

Details are released of the new twin-rotor **helicopter** ordered for the RAF. It can carry 19 when used as an ambulance, and cruise at 92mph with a piston engine or 138mph with a gas turbine engine.

■ The owners of 3 Canadian fishing vessels are fined $100 each for having no Ohio fishing licences, and $200 each for using illegal nets, by the municipal court at Ashtabula, Ohio, after pleading guilty to illegal fishing by poaching in Lake Erie's American waters.

5 Saturday

Manchester City win the F A Cup *(see panel)*.

■ A female **coelacanth** weighing about 160lbs, caught on Thursday night off the Comoro Islands, in the Indian Ocean, is taken in a special military aircraft to Tananarive, Madagascar. The fish contains eggs, but scientists can't tell whether the fish lays them, or gives birth to live fish.

. . . 70°F in Channel Islands, and from Kent to Norfolk, including London Airport. Jersey has 13.2hrs of sunshine . . .

6 Sunday

Fishermen who use the port of Pwllheli, Caernarvonshire, sign a **petition** objecting to the appointment of an Englishman as harbourmaster. They want a Welsh-speaking Welshman.

■ 2,000 soldiers and **civil defence** workers stand down this weekend after Exercise Try-out, in which a 10-megaton H-bomb was assumed to have dropped on London. The exercise was to test the help the army could give the civil authorities in the event of a nuclear attack.

■ Two Oxford undergraduates, both Rhodes Scholars, successfully walk from London to Oxford in less than 24hrs. They leave Marble Arch at 5am and arrive at Magdalen Bridge at 9.30pm.

7 Monday

Plans are unveiled in New York for a new Guggenheim Museum, to hold the collection of the late Solomon R Guggenheim. Designed by **Frank Lloyd Wright,** it will have an interior ramp ¾-mile long, with walls leaning slightly outward, and will take about 2yrs to build.

■ The British government grants £26,000 to help starving tribesmen in the **Aden** Protectorate. £10,000 goes to farmers in the Bethan area – their crops were ruined by frost. The rest is for nomads, whose flocks are dying after a 3yr drought, and for the replacement of central grain stocks.

■ A Swiss airman has landed a **helicopter** on a narrow rock ledge on the Furggen ridge of the Matterhorn, at 10,500ft. A photographer was able to get out and climb to the upper station of the Brenil Furggjoch cable railway, where he found the bodies of two Italian climbers killed during a snowstorm on March 20. They are frozen in, and can't be freed until the summer thaw.

8 Tuesday

Eighty-eight double-decker and 38 single-decker **London buses** will be fitted with amber flashing light traffic indicators at the rear and over their driving mirrors. Semaphore arm indicators aren't strong enough for the work.

■ To show how quickly homes could be provided, employees of Barnsley Corporation's direct building department complete two three-bedroomed houses 11 days after the first bricks are laid. 30,000 bricks were laid in 32hrs, and 1,848 tiles in 27hrs. The houses are now painted and ready for occupation.

■ *Look Back in Anger* by **John Osborne** *above,* opens at the Royal Court Theatre, London. Most critics dislike it, but KennethTynan says it is the 'best young play of the decade'.

9 Wednesday

Susan, a 7 week-old 8lb 3oz **tiger cub** born at London Zoo in March, is on show for the first time. She was abandoned by her mother, Nepti, and raised by her keepers and a boxer dog.

■ Prime Minister **Sir Anthony Eden** refuses to enlarge on his statement about Commander Crabb (see page 38).

■ **Louis 'Satchmo' Armstrong** plays a special number, *Mahogany Hall Stomp,* 'for one of my fans', at a concert at the Empress Hall. The fan is **Princess Margaret** who is at the concert with a group of friends.

10 Thursday

New Moon

Local elections give **Labour** a gain of 186 seats. Liberals gain 5, but the Conservatives

Homes Hit as Secret RAF Bomber Crashes

MAY 11

A top-secret RAF Valiant JET BOMBER, designed to carry nuclear weapons, crashes into a railway embankment at Southwick, Sussex. The wreckage showers houses and the main London-Brighton railway track. Four people are injured and 3 crewmen killed, but a fourth bales out safely.

and the Independents lose 191.

■ **Sir Winston Churchill** receives the Charlemagne prize in Aachen, for services to European unity.

■ The case of the **missing rabbits** of Aschaffenburg, which has baffled some of Bavaria's best-known detectives, has been solved. The rabbits were stolen from a teacher, who set his pupils an essay on 'Our favourite Sunday meal'. Two boys described the roasted rabbits they had eaten the Sunday before. The thief has been sent to prison for a year.

11 Friday

A top-secret RAF **Valiant jet bomber** crashes (See panel above).

■ The Russians say that sailors on board the *Ordjonikidz* (see page 38) had seen a **frogman** approach the vessel.

■ 1,000 miners are **sacked** at two 'trouble' pits, East and Steer pits at Gwaun-cae-Gurwen, Glam. They went back to work yesterday after the latest 14-day strike.

12 Saturday

Hungary frees more than 100 politicians, including the 50 Social Democrats Hugh Gaitskell had on the list he tried to give Soviet leader Nikita Khruschev at a dinner during his recent visit.

■ Film star **Montgomery Clift,** 35, *(below)*, is seriously injured in a car crash after leaving a dinner party given by Michael Wilding and Elizabeth Taylor in Hollywood. Wilding, Rock Hudson and others pull Clift out of the wreckage. He has concussion, facial cuts and a broken nose.

13 Sunday

Russia announces that **concentration camps** will be abolished within the next 18 months. A commission will revise cases of those sentenced for political and counter-revolutionary crimes. It should 'fully rehabilitate innocent people by October'.

■ **Stirling Moss** wins the Monaco Grand Prix for the second time. Driving a Maserati, he makes virtually all the running in the gruelling 200-mile race.

14 Monday

A **swan** on the tracks stops a Waterloo-bound train outside Kingston, Surrey. Swan keeper Richard Turk (80) is called to rescue the bird and puts the swan back in the river.

■ All 11,000 Standard workers are back at work pending talks about 3,500 proposed **sackings** caused by the introduction of automation in the tractor factory.

■ A bronze statue of **Pinocchio** is unveiled in Collodi, Tuscany, in the presence of Italy's President Gronchi.

15 Tuesday

British Rail buy 250 tickets for the First Test against Australia at Trent Bridge, Nottingham.They'll sell 50 tickets each day of the 5-day match (starts June 7) for 12s. each to the first fans queuing to buy cheap day returns within a 70 mile radius of Nottingham.

■ A factory making a powder used in the manufacture of plastics, rubber, paint and wallpaper and run by robots, opens in Derby. Machines do everything, and only five men at a time are needed to watch them.

■ The breakdown of talks in London on **Singapore independence** within the Commonwealth, as Britain can't find a way of ensuring that the island will never become Communist. (Singapore is a big British naval base).

10-Wicket Laker Has The Aussies in a Spin

JIM LAKER (34) takes all 10 Australian wickets for 88 runs at the Oval. The England off-spinner bowls a marathon stint of 4½ hrs and the crowd gives him a standing ovation. Later in the series, at Old Trafford in July, Laker equals his remarkable feat, going on to take 19 wickets in the match.

Laker and team-mates Cox and wicketkeeper Swetman appeal to the umpire, and the last Aussie batsman, Wilson, is on his way back to the pavilion – and Laker into the record books for his ten-wicket haul at the Oval. Left: It's O J Laker! Gentleman Jim celebrates his incredible feat with a pint of orange juice.

16 Wednesday

Reports of a romance between **Princess Margaret** (25) and Christian of Hanover (36), brother of the Duke of Brunswick and Queen Frederika of Greece, are officially denied.

■ Off-spinner **Jim Laker** (34) takes all 10 Australian wickets at the Oval *(see panel)*.

■ Britain detonates a fourth **atom bomb** in the Monte Bello islands off Western Australia.

17 Thursday

Noel Coward, travelling from Jamaica to France, stays on board when his liner calls at Plymouth – he's afraid the Inland Revenue will get him. Last year he had to pay £25,000 in tax after an 8-week stay.

■ Three RAF squadrons equipped with Valiants are ordered not to fly pending an enquiry into the plane crash on May 11 at Southwick, nr Brighton, Sussex.

■ The Brussels newspaper *Het Volk* reports that **Princess Alexandra** (19), daughter of the Duchess of Kent, is engaged to King Baudoin of Belgium. Official denials are issued in both countries.

■ The terrorists in **Cyprus** accuse the governor of hiding the true number of British troop casualties, for fear of public opinion in Britain. The official British death toll is 31, but the terrorists claim that 151 soldiers have been killed, and 217 wounded.

18 Friday

A **garden party** is held in St James's Square, London, for about 300 staff from the Ministry of Labour so that the Minister, **Iain**

Macleod, can meet some of the people who work for him.

■ **National Service** call-up ends for grade 3 men, but those already serving must complete their time.

■ The **Coal Board** refuses to reverse its decision despite pleas by the NUM on behalf of the 1,000 miners sacked from pits at Gwaun-cae-Gurwen, Glam. on May 11. The pits will close next Saturday.

19 Saturday

Whitsun Bank Holiday

A **BOAC stratocruiser,** flying from London to New York with 38 passengers on board, comes down at Stretton Royal Naval Base, nr Warrington, Lancs, instead of Burtonwood Airport, 5 miles away, where it is due to pick up a passenger. The pilot realises he is in the wrong place and takes off again at once.

■ Holiday motorists in France are held up by road blocks and **traffic jams** organised by peasants and small farmers, drawing attention to their grievances against the government.

■ A Przewalski **foal** is born at Whipsnade Zoo for the first time in 20yrs. The parents of the baby Mongolian wild horse came to the zoo originally from Portugal as part of an exchange of animals.

20 Sunday

New Moon

The Americans drop the **first H-bomb** from a plane. The bomb is released at 50,000ft by a 600mph jet bomber and explodes at an altitude of 10,000ft over Namu Island, Bikini Atoll, in the Pacific. The flash is seen 1,000 miles away.

■ Twenty people are **killed** or injured at the Grand Prix des Frontières, Chimay, Belgium, when Swiss driver Maurice Caillet's Maserati touches the Tojiero-Bristol of Christopher Threlfall (GB) who is in the lead. The Maserati shoots off the track in flames.

■ London airport and airline staff are alerted when ticking is heard from a **suitcase**. When the owner is found, he takes a toy car out of the suitcase; the mechanism had gone off by mistake.

■ **Sir Max Beerbohm** (83), author and caricaturist, dies at Rapallo, Italy, his home for 40yrs. A month before his death, he married German-born Elizabeth Jungmann, his secretary for many years

21 Monday

Bank Holiday

Most main roads from the coast are affected by **heavy traffic** and there is a 70 mile traffic jam from Folkestone, Kent, to London.

■ Fifty soldiers **escape** from a smoke-filled army transit shelter, when fire breaks out 150ft under ground at Tottenham Court Road, London.

STIRLING SILVER!

Britain's Stirling Moss, driving a Maserati, enjoys world-wide success. In January 40,000 see him win the New Zealand Grand Prix *(right)*. In May he adds the German 1,000 km race at Nurburgring.

■ Funding for **books in schools** is inadequate, says primary school head Edward Homer, of Wirral, Cheshire, at the National Association of Head Teachers' conference at Brighton. Some local authorities only spend an average of 5s. 9½d. on text books for each primary school child, and 15s. a year for each secondary school child.

22 Tuesday

Thirty-six **firemen collapse** in the intense heat and stifling smoke of a fire 150ft below London in a disused underground tunnel and are brought out at Goodge St tube station. Fifteen men are rescued by a human chain of 200 firemen passing them up 250 steps. The fire is being fought by 500 firemen from every station in London.
It takes more than 24hrs to put it out.
■ Swedish film star **Anita 'the iceberg' Ekberg**, marries British actor **Anthony Steel** at the Palazzo Vecchio, Florence, Italy. She wears no hat, gloves or stockings with her white dress, which leaves one shoulder bare, but she carries a small bouquet and paints her nails silver. At the reception the pair cut a 6-tier wedding cake with an antique sword. (Picture, page 33).

23 Wednesday

Calder Hall atomic energy power station, *(below)*, the first to supply electricity from nuclear energy, is switched on.
■ The Navy is lending a cruiser and two frigates to make a film about the escape of HMS *Amethyst* from the Yangtse River, China, in 1949. The film will be made in Hong Kong and will star **Richard Todd**. HMS *Amethyst* made a daring 150-mile night time escape, bombarded all the way by Communists on both sides of the river.

24 Thursday
Full Moon

Potato wholesalers in London want the government to persuade people to eat more potatoes – consumption is down after a successful appeal for economy during the shortage. They say they can't get rid of 100,000 tons of old potatoes imported during the recent shortages and they are now rotting at the docks.

■ The Russians can still hear the **BBC** – the jamming of broadcasts was stopped during Bulganin and Khruschev's visit to Britain in April, and it hasn't been resumed.

■ Railway police are searching for £200 in new **silver coins** missing from a London-Bognor Regis train. They were being sent straight from the Mint to a bank in Bognor in a special transit drum.

25 Friday

For 10yrs, 62 disabled ex-servicemen, mostly World War I **veterans** in a home in Worthing, got money at Christmas, a coach trip each summer, and a packet of cigarettes each once a fortnight. Now the men know who their anonymous 'fairy godmother' was. Miss Gladys Walton (67), of High Salvington nr Worthing, died 3 months ago and in her will she has left each of them £100.

■ A possible **reprieve** for the two coal pits at Gwaun-cae-Gurwen, Glam. The Coal Board say that if 285 miners work a trial week and bring up enough coal, more men will be taken on. Within a month all could be at work again. Local miners' leaders are picking the 'commando' squad which will try to save the pits today.

26 Saturday

Scientists have been asked to find a paint **woodpeckers** won't like, so that it can be used on electricity poles in the Midlands, which have been attacked by the birds.

■ Millions of **mice** driven from the fields by exceptionally heavy rain have invaded central New South Wales, Australia. The rodents have eaten their way into fridges, and chewed registration plates from cars. Supplies of poison have run out, and out-breaks of disease are feared.

27 Sunday

A **wall of flame** roars through the forest nr Wareham, Dorset. At the nearby village of Sandford, flames are stopped only 200 yds from the houses. Hundreds of firemen and troops fight this blaze – and 6 other heath fires – hampered by shortages of water, and burning telegraph poles that fall and block the roads.

28 Monday

A **downpour** in the West puts out the last of the fires that burned over the weekend. In Cornwall, ¾in rain falls, almost all in 5 mins.

■ **The Queen** is guarded by a huge security force when she goes to a military parade in London. Intelligence reports from Cyprus report that terrorist gunmen may have landed in Britain.

■ **Weevils** have attacked 40,000 trees in Sherwood Forest. The weevil larvae suck the sap, killing the trees. Infected trees are being felled to avoid the damage spreading.

29 Tuesday

■ **President Eisenhower** asks Congress for an extra $82,500,000 for the Atomic Energy Commission, to design, develop and produce new weapons, and speed up the development of civil power. It is also considering a request for $1,672,000,000 to build new atomic energy plants.

. . . Josephine, 1 of only 2 whooping cranes in captivity, hatches 1 of her 2 eggs at Audubon Park, New Orleans, USA. The birds are very rare – there may only be 30 in the world . . .

30 Wednesday

In the **Birthday Honours** list, **Len Hutton** is knighted, **Professor Arnold Toynbee** becomes a Companion of Honour, **Peggy Ashcroft** becomes a DBE, **Pat Smythe** gains the OBE, Anthony Powell the CBE, and **Anthony Blunt** (curator of the Queen's pictures) becomes a KCVO.

■ Agreement in Venice by 6 of the European governments of the Coal and Steel Committee to discuss a draft treaty establishing a common market.

31 Thursday

Union Day, South Africa

Bush pilot Carl Crossley (60), who has been stranded on a 10ft ice floe in Hudson's Bay, Canada, for 12 days, is **rescued**. He has lived under a tarpaulin from his plane, eating dates, oatmeal, raw beef and powdered milk.

■ Two copper **Dead Sea Scrolls**, found in caves at Qumran, Jordan, and cut open and deciphered in Manchester, contain lists of 60 hoards of treasure buried in an area stretching from Hebron to Nablus, 50 miles north, involving nearly 200 tons of gold and silver. The exact locations are hard to identify, as the land has changed a lot since the1st century AD.

■ May has been a very **dry** month. Large areas of the country have had only half the average rainfall. London has had just 0.23ins rain compared with 1896 when just 0.16 ins rain fell.

ANOTHER CUP FOR STAN!

Stanley Matthews, an FA Cup winner at last in 1953, continues to pick up silverware – this time for tennis. He wins the men's singles and doubles at the South Shore club, Blackpool. And there are trophies for daughter Jean (left) and son Stanley. Earlier this year Stan was recalled to the England soccer team.

JUNE

1 Friday

Eckington Parish Council (Derbyshire) bans

BUCK RYAN – THE CARTOON ADVENTURES

In the Police laboratory, a bullet from Mark Thyme's revolver is fired into a padded catchment box
P47
It is then compared with the bullet retrieved from the murdered Coastguard
SCORING MARKS ARE IDENTICAL, MR RYAN. I'LL HAVE THEM PHOTOGRAPHED
THANKS, CHUM. NOW I MUST FIND OUT WHY MARK THYME KILLED THAT COASTGUARD
BACK TO THE SAXONSEA POLICE STATION, ZOLA
D'YOU MIND IF I TAKE TIME OFF FOR A HAIR 'DO', BUCK? I FEEL A BIT WINDSWEPT

dogs from meetings. One councillor protests: she's been accompanied by her collie to all meetings since 1947.

■ **Josephine** the whooping crane, who hatched one egg 3 days ago, successfully hatches her second egg The world whooping crane population is now 32.

■ **New Zealand**'s Minister of Railways offers permanent employment to some of the 2,640 workers laid off by Standard Motors, Coventry, if they can pay their fare out and find housing.

2 Saturday

Keepers at Belle Vue Zoo, Manchester, go on a 'no cleaning' strike. They want double time for Bank Holiday and Sunday working, a fortnight's paid holiday, and an increase in basic earnings. The strike is later called off.

■ The **Duke of Gloucester** unveils a memorial at Groesbeek, Netherlands, commemorating the 1,103 officers and men of the British Commonwealth forces who fell during the advance from the Seine into Germany during World War II and who have no known grave.

3 Sunday

British Rail abolishes third class travel. First and second classes are amalgamated into first class, and the old third class becomes second class.

■ **Dresden**'s 750th anniversary is celebrated with the reopening of the Semper Gallery, displaying many valuable paintings returned from Russia. It has taken 10yrs work to rebuild Dresden, after its destruction by Allied air raids in World War II.

4 Monday

The 6-month-old dispute at the **Cammell Laird** shipyard, Birkenhead, over who should drill holes in panels has finally been settled: the shipwrights, not the woodworkers, drill the holes.

■ The Egyptian government representative on the **Suez Canal** Company's board says that Egypt will not extend the company's 99-year concession, which ends in 1968.

So Farewell, Then . . . Some Who Died in '56

Princess Marie Louise
Bela Lugosi
Robert Newton
Tommy Dorsey
Walter de la Mare
Michael Arlen
Berthold Brecht
Clarence Birdseye
Mistinguett
Sir Max Beerbohm
A A Milne
Lord Trenchard
H L Mencken

DRACULA is with us no more . . . well, Bela Lugosi (above). Also departed (below, from left): Berthold Brecht, the playwright; Clarence Birdseye, of frozen food fame; bandleader Tommy Dorsey; and (bottom) singer Mistinguett.

■ **The Queen** leaves Teesport, nr Middlesborough, on the royal yacht *Britannia* for an official visit to **Sweden** which will take in the Equestrian Olympic Games.

5 Tuesday
Full Moon

Water restrictions are imposed in Liverpool and Carlisle. Liverpool's reservoirs are at a record low. There'll be a £5 fine imposed on anyone using a hosepipe.
■ Dutch dealers refuse to take back about 65,000 tons of unsold **potatoes** sent to Britain last April during the potato shortage.
■ **Segregation** on city buses in Montgomery, Alabama, is ruled unconstitutional by a Federal Court, but the date of the judgement has been postponed for 2 weeks to allow the parties involved to appeal. Blacks in Montgomery have been boycotting the buses for 6 months.

6 Wednesday

Lavandin, ridden by W R Johnstone, wins the **Derby** at Epsom in rain and wind.
■ Britain's new turbo-prop airliner, the **Vanguard**, will be a double-decker, and will carry 115 passengers, on 95% of the world's major air routes, at up to 425mph. The first Vanguard is due to fly in 1958.
■ All naval establishments at **Scapa Flow** will close, except for an oil depot, says the Admiralty.

7 Thursday

The **Wimbledon** tennis championships will be televised this year, and for the next 4yrs, by both the BBC and ITV says the All England Club.
■ The population of the Soviet Union is 200 million according to *Pravda* – smaller than expected. It's the first official Soviet figure since the 1939 census.
■ Singer **Paul Robeson** has again been denied a passport by the American State Department. He's been trying to get one since 1953, but he refuses to sign an affidavit saying he has never been a member of the Communist party, or to attend a State Department hearing on his application.

8 Friday
New Moon

US **President Eisenhower** is taken ill in the night with ilietis, the partial obstruction of the small intestine He has a successful operation to remove the blockage.
■ Chelmsford railway station, Essex, celebrates its 100th birthday with decorations and an exhibition of railway history in the local library. The newly-**electrified line** between Chelmsford and Liverpool Street will open on Monday.
■ **Norfolk Island**, between Australia and New Zealand, celebrates the centenary of the arrival at Kingston of the descendants of the *Bounty* mutineers – the 8 families who left barren, overcrowded Pitcairn Island for the new home on Norfolk Island given to them by Queen Victoria.

9 Saturday

Police in Ormskirk, Lancs, appeal to men and boys over 16 to have their fingerprints taken, to help solve the **murder** of two elderly sisters found battered to death on May 6.
■ Sixty-two **Japanese prisoners** arrive home today after 10yrs' internment in Siberia. More than half are ill, and 27 go straight to hospital when their ship, the *Hokuto Maru*, docks at Maizuru. In the group is General Otozo Yamada, commandedr of Japanese forces in Manchuria during World War II.

10 Sunday

The **Duke of Edinburgh**'s birthday. He's 35.
■ The **Equestrian Olympics** start in Stockholm, with a parade of the nine competing nations.
■ A parade in honour of the Queen's birthday is held at Kure, Japan, by Commonwealth forces – the

BRITAIN STRIKE OLYMPIC GOLD

The Queen watches with pride as the British team wins the gold medal in the 3-day event at the Stockholm Equestrian Olympics. Weldon, Hill and Rook are pictured during the medals' ceremony. The event is held separately from the summer Games, which are taking place in Sydney, Australia, in the autumn.

final event here before it closes down. Kure was one of the biggest British bases in the world during the Korean war.

■ Supporters of the deposed dictator **General Peron** revolt in Argentina. Martial law is declared, and all civil and commercial flights are stopped for 24hrs. The rebellion lasts just one day.

11 Monday

The first survey vessel designed especially for the Antarctic, the royal research ship *John Biscoe*, is launched in Paisley. The 2,500 ton diesel-electric ship, has ice-breaker bows and full heating and insulation against the Antarctic weather.

■ A welcome home for 7 British scientists who have spent 6 months compiling a detailed survey of uninhabited Gough Island in the South Atlantic, 1,500 miles from Cape Town and 250 miles from Tristan da Cunha.

■ All traffic is banned in the mountains of West **Cyprus** as 5,000 troops take part in the search for the rebel leader Dighenis (believed to be George Grivas) and his henchmen. Dighenis has a price of £10,000 on his head.

12 Tuesday

At their conference in Bridlington, Yorks, the National Federation of **Old Age Pensioners** calls for pensions of £3 a week and a bonus to meet the increased cost of living.

■ Father Kallinikos Macheriotis, senior archimandrite at All Saint's Greek Orthodox Church, Camden Town, London is **deported** to Athens. He supports the ENOSIS movement in Cyprus, and it's suggested that he has collected money from the Greek community to send to the terrorists.

■ Work starts on the **first motorway** in Britain – the Preston, Lancs, by-pass. It will be 8 ½ miles long, and will have one access point. It will eventually become part of the Birmingham-Shap motorway.

■ The record for walking from Oxford to Cambridge, set last Saturday, is broken by 4 Cambridge undergraduates, who cover the 79 miles in 19hrs 16mins.

13 Wednesday

Holidaymakers at Bridlington, Yorks, must pay 3d. a session (morning, afternoon, or evening) to use their own deckchairs.

■ The Oxford to Cambridge walking record is broken again – less than 24hrs after the previous record was set. The new record time is 17hr 56min for the 79 miles.

■ Another **dispute** over drilling holes at Cammell Laird's shipyard, Birkenhead. 150 joiners strike when drillers are given a job on metal with asbestos sheets attached.

. . . The last British troops leave Suez. Cheers break out when the Egyptian flag is raised . . .

14 Thursday

A new development plan for the area round St Paul's, designed by Sir William Holford, is accepted in principle by the City of London.

■ Fourteen inmates of the Ohio State penitentiary, chosen from 134 volunteers, some serving life sentences, are innoculated with **live cancer cells** in an experiment to find out how the body of a person without cancer destroys implanted cancer cells.

15 Friday

The **Prime Minister** says that at a time when the government is calling for restraint over pay, it would be wrong for MPs 'who are rightly expected to set an example' to increase their own.

■ After a second week's **test mining**, the Coal Board announce that the two coal pits at Gwaun-cae-Gurwen, Glam. will stay open, and another 300 men will be taken on.

■ **Polio** vaccinations are stopped in Macclesfield, Ches., after 5 cases of the disease are reported, and one child dies. Diphtheria and whooping cough immunisations are also stopped.

16 Saturday

The American vice-consul in Nicosia is killed, and 3 other US diplomats wounded, when a **bomb** is thrown into a restaurant. The vice-consul had only been in Cyprus a month.

■ The Chief of the Clan Cameron, Lieut. Col. Donald Hamish Cameron, welcomes 1,000 men and women from all over the world to Achnacarry, Inverness-shire, for the first world gathering of the Clan Cameron since 1938. It's only the second major assembly of Cameron men since 800 volunteers joined Bonnie Prince Charlie at Glenfinnan in 1745.

17 Sunday

Britain wins the **bronze medal** for the team show jumping at the Equestrian Olympics in Stockholm – Germany wins gold, and Italy silver.

■ Over 2,000 men are fighting over 90 **forest fires** in northern Ontario, Canada. Thousands of acres are in flames, and 25 fires are out of control. Lightning has started 170 fires in the last 4 days. Water bombs are dropped from planes.

■ British troops searching western **Cyprus** have captured a gang of 7 EOKA terrorists, though Grivas has escaped. The search has been hampered by a serious forest fire in the Troodos mountains.

18 Monday

Derbyshire Fire Brigade is called out to capture a 6ft **boa constrictor**, loose in the kitchen of Mrs Annie Cheetham, of Chaddesden. It takes two volunteers 20mins to catch it. The special services committee will consider the fee, as it's the first time they've dealt with this sort of emergency.

■ The **Chancellor** says people can hold up to £500 of premium bonds, not just £250 as announced in the Budget.

. . . America wins the Wightman Cup, beating Britain by 5 matches to 2 . . .

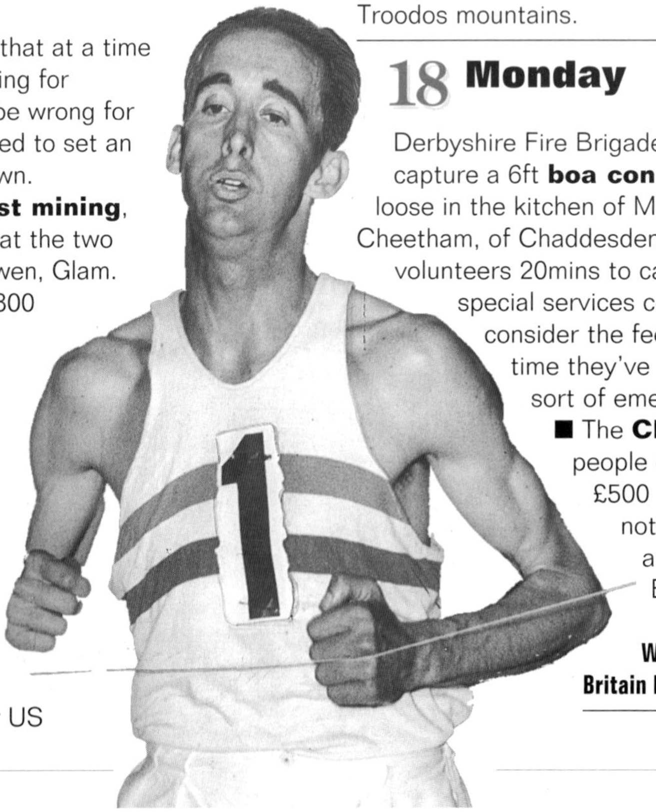

19 Tuesday

The opening of **Royal Ascot**.
■ **Gordon Pirie** *(below, facing page)* sets a new **world record** for the 5,000 metres in Bergen, Norway, of 13 mins 36.8secs, beating the old record by 3.8secs.
■ A senior manager at the Royal Maternity Hospital, Glasgow, finds the bodies of 35 **stillborn children** in a tea-chest in the mortuary. The bodies, which should have been buried immediately, must have taken up to two months to accumulate. The police and the hospital have launched enquiries.

NASSER TAKES COMMAND IN EGYPT

20 Wednesday

A Venezuelan Super **Constellation airliner** with 64 passengers and 10 crew members on board crashes in flames in the Atlantic 32 miles east of Asbury Park, New Jersey. It left Idlewild Airport, New York, 2hrs earlier, but turned back after developing engine trouble. It is jettisoning fuel to prepare for landing when it hurtles into the sea. There are no survivors.
■ Liverpool City Councillor Lawrence Murphy (38) is **sacked** from his job as a furniture salesman because he's wearing a grey pullover under his black jacket. The staff were told last week that it was against the rules to wear pullovers on duty.

21 Thursday

The existence of a new atomic particle – the **neutrino** – is announced by the US Atomic Energy Commission.
■ Hotels in Southport, Lancs, are refusing to take guests from Macclesfield after a woman from there died of **polio** last Tuesday. There have been 8 cases of polio reported in Macclesfield.
■ A helicopter rescues a sick, motherless **baby elephant**, weighing 200 lbs, from the Malayan jungle. The starving elephant, about a fortnight old, wandered into a remote jungle fort at Telanok in Pahang State, and the next day, milk, babies' bottles, medicine and the State game warden flew in. An RAF Whirlwind is flying it to Kuala Lumpur.

22 Friday

The Food Standards Committee proposes legally fixed standards for **sausages:** a minimum meat content of 65% for pork sausages, and 50% for other meat sausages, with not more than half the meat content to be fat.
■ **Stroma** in the Pentland Firth is to lose its only shop – last Thursday John Sinclair (45), the manager, left for the mainland, and assistant Jessie Smith (40) goes in a week. The remaining 50 inhabitants will have to have food sent from Wick – 18 miles by road and a 2 mile sea crossing.
■ Australians are warned not to drink **rainwater**, in case it contains radio-active dust from the last British atom test at Monte Bello yesterday.
. . . Poet and novelist Walter de la Mare (83) dies at his home in Twickenham . . .

23 Saturday

New Moon

Colonel Gamal Abdel Nasser *(above)* is elected President of Egypt: voting is

compulsory and there is only one candidate.
■ The Queen reviews the **Grenadier Guards**, of which she is Colonel-in-Chief, at Windsor Castle, as part of their 300th anniversary celebrations.The Grenadiers came into being in 1656 as the Royal Regiment of Guards in Bruges, Belgium.
■ Novelist **Michael Arlen** (60), an Armenian born Dikran Kouyoumdjian at Rustchuk, Bulgaria and naturalised British in 1922, dies in New York. His most famous book is *The Green Hat*.

24 Sunday

Mike Hawthorne and **Peter Collins**, driving a Ferrari, win the Italian Grand Prix at Monza, at an average speed of 121mph. Stirling Moss in a Maserati is second.
■ Stewards can't control the crowd at Wentworth for Britain's first Sunday golf spectacle. Only about 1 in 50 can see the great **Ben Hogan**. Several spectators suffer minor injuries, and the stewards have to send for ropes and more helpers.
■ Four members of RAF Transport Command HQ, Upavon, Wilts, cut 14½hrs from the 51½hr record for the 90-mile row from Pewsey, Wilts, to Christchurch, Hants, along the River Avon. They left Pewsey at 4.30am on Saturday and took 36hr 10min to row to the open sea at Christchurch.

25 Monday

■ A service is held in Westminster Abbey for 300 **VC holders**, as part of the centenary celebrations.
■ Australian Prime Minister and cricket fanatic **Robert Menzies**, in town for the Commonwealth Conference, has a TV in the back of his car, so that he can watch the 2nd Test Match as he is driven across London.
■ Opening of the Wimbledon tennis championships: former champion **Jaroslav Drobny** (35), who won the men's title in 1954, is knocked out in the first round by Ramanath Krishnan (19) of India.
■ All British officials in **Cyprus** are warned of the danger of assassination, after Judge Bernard Shaw (65), who has imposed 6 of the 7 death sentences on terrorists, is shot by 2 gunmen when his car is held up in heavy traffic in Nicosia.

26 Tuesday

The centenary of the **Victoria Cross** *(See panel, above)*.
■ A court in Bodmin, Cornwall, hears that Harriet Richards (72), a gypsy with 14 children, sold farmer Leslie Osborne (44), for £600, a '**magic carpet**' which would give him and his wife 3 wishes, and promised she'd remove evil spells from his farm. She's fined £100 and put on probation for 3yrs.

QUEEN MEETS THE VICTORIA CROSS HEROES

The centenary of the VICTORIA CROSS. The Queen reviews a parade of 300 holders, some in wheelchairs, in Hyde Park, followed by a garden party at Marlborough House. Among the holders are 6ft 5in Bill Speakman, who won his VC in Korea, and the 5ft 3in Australian 'devil in a slouched hat' Jim Woods, who won his VC in France in 1918, both pictured, left.

27 Wednesday

Watched by a crowd of visitors, Wally Swain (60) a keeper at London Zoo, locks himself in a serval's cage to **rescue** a baby thrush. He doesn't take in the usual broom in case he needs to fend off the 2ft high, 2ft 6in long African wild cat, as there isn't time. He's unharmed, and the thrush hops into the shrubbery.

■ The government **robot** ACE – Automatic Computing Engine – a calculator which cost £40,000 and has been in use 6yrs at the National Physical Laboratory, Teddington, Middx, where it was used on problems involving A-bombs, guided rockets and taxation changes, is being pensioned off to the Science Museum, London.

■ The British Motor Corporation announces nearly 6,000 employees will be **sacked** tomorrow with a week's wages in lieu of notice, because of falling car sales. Many more of the 55,000 employees will be put onto 3 and 4-day weeks.

■ Tiny the **sea lion** has a female calf, the first born at London Zoo for 22yrs. Tiny and her mate, Bill, have had 3 other calves, all male – they have all been moved to Whipsnade as Bill will not tolerate another male in his pool.

Many Killed as Workers Riot in Poland

There is rioting in Poznan, Poland. Striking workers pull down the Russian flag, overturn trams, attack the HQ of the Communist Party, and set fire to the prison. It's the biggest anti-communist demonstration since the East German uprising of June, 1953. There are thousands of foreign visitors in Poznan for a trade fair at which 20 British firms are exhibiting.

28 Thursday

Riots in Poznan *(See panel above)*.
■ **Bobby Wilson**, the last British man left in Wimbledon, is knocked out by Neale Fraser of Australia, 8-6, 7-5, 6-3. Wilson had beaten former champion Budge Patty on Wednesday.

29 Friday

Poznan, Poland has been cordoned off by tanks and is under a dusk to dawn curfew.
■ The West German newspaper *Bild* publishes a report speculating that **Commander Crabb**, who disappeared last April, is in a Soviet gaol. The paper says Crabb, had been caught by Soviet frogmen, and was promised his freedom and £1,000 a month if he would work for Soviet naval intelligence for 10yrs – Crabb had refused.
■ Playwright and intellectual **Arthur Miller** (his work includes *Death Of A Salesman* and *The View From The Bridge)* marries film star **Marilyn Monroe** in New York.

30 Saturday

The worst **disaster** in civil aviation history when two US airliners collide in a thunderstorm over the Grand Canyon in Arizona. A total of 128 die: there are no survivors.
■ Scores of Ministry of Labour officers are sent to the Birmingham area to help find new jobs for the 6,000 men **sacked** from BMC.

JULY

1 Sunday

Polish security police question 323 people arrested during the **Poznan riots**. Thousands of Poles attend a service in Brompton Oratory, London, in memory of the Poznan dead. The official death toll so far is 48, but British businessmen returning from a trade fair say nearer 200 is more likely.
■ **Peter Collins**, driving a Ferrari, wins the French Grand Prix at Reims. He now has an undisputed lead in this year's world championship.

2 Monday

Racehorse owner **Rachel Parsons** (71), *right*, reputed to be one of the 5 richest people in the country, is found dead with head injuries at her home in Newmarket.
A qualified engineer, her passion has been breeding and racing horses. Dennis James Pratt (21), an unemployed stableman, is charged with her murder.

■ Lebanon nationalises a vital 20-mile stretch of **oil pipeline** that belongs to the Iraq Petroleum Co. There is no mention of compensation. The Lebanese now want as much for their 20 miles of pipeline as Syria gets for 263 miles – £6 million p.a.

3 Tuesday

Col. Ivan Bubchikov, an assistant military attaché at the Russian embassy in Washington, USA, is expelled. He was caught **stealing** American military correspondence from a letter box.

■ Sixty children under 5 are **sent home** from the Lancastrian Council School, Tottenham, after two children are admitted to hospital with polio. The nursery wing will be closed for 3 weeks, but 200 older children at the school will continue to attend classes.

■ American tennis star **Beverly Fleitz** (26) scratches from Wimbledon. She thought she had a touch of 'flu, but she is pregnant. Her erstwhile opponent, Angela Buxton, will now play Pat Ward, so there'll be a British girl in the final for the first time since 1939.

4 Wednesday

Jean Margett (18), of Sunnyvale, California, is found alive in the wreck of a car that plunged 300ft into Parley's Canyon, nr Salt Lake City, Utah, 9 days ago. Her fiancé, James Hixon (22) is dead. They were returning from a fishing trip when the accident happened. The car was only spotted last night.

■ Union leaders in the iron and steel industry call a **strike** of 14,000 men, to start on July 14. Employers have refused to increase an offer of 10s. a week. Maintenance men – all craftsmen – want more because they say their skill isn't properly recognised.

5 Thursday

Poland rejects the American Red Cross offer of food for Poznan, made through the League of Red Crosses in Geneva.

■ **Judge Bernard Shaw**, who was shot by two Cypriot terrorists on June 25, returns to the bench to resume the trial of two boys accused of throwing bombs. They are among the people who applaud him when he says, 'I'm a tough old bird'.

■ There are 120 competitors in this year's **Tour de France** cycle race which starts today at Reims.

. . . American composer Harry Link (60), whose hits include *These Foolish Things* **and** *I've Got a Feeling I'm Falling*, **dies in New York . . .**

6 Friday

Playwright **Arthur Miller**, having denied that he was a member of the Communist Party, is granted a passport for 6 months by the American State Department – he'll be able to honeymoon in Britain with **Marilyn Monroe**, whom he married on June 29.

■ Animal expert **Barbara Woodhouse**, *above*, starts residential training courses for badly-behaved dogs and their owners in her 40-bedroom manor house at Croxley Green, Herts. The courses cost 8gns.

Hoad Beats Rosewall to Land Title at Wimbledon

Australian LEW HOAD (21) wins the men's singles title at Wimbledon, beating his fellow-countryman and doubles partner Ken Rosewall (21) 6-2, 4-6, 7-5, 6-4.
SHIRLEY FRY (USA) beats Angela Buxton (GB), 6-3, 6-1 in the Ladies' Singles.

■ The makers of **4711 cologne** are taking legal action against Herr Koelsch of Seigen, Germany, on the grounds that he is damaging their business. Koelsch empties cess pits, and his phone number – 4711 – is prominently displayed on his van. He says he got the phone number by chance, and it's his right to display it on his van.
. . . It's 80°F at Kew and Southend, 85°F in Jersey – the first time it has hit the 80s this year . . .

7 Saturday

The first British woman is killed in **Cyprus**, when Greek Cypriot terrorists shoot customs official George Kaberry (33) and his wife Marjorie – they arrived on the island in February, and were ambushed on their way to a picnic.
■ A *Madonna and Child* painted in 1453 by **Jan van Eyck**, the most valuable painting in the National Gallery of Victoria, reaches London on the liner *Otranto*. The Australians have lent it to an exhibition in Bruges, Belgium, and it will later go on show in the National Gallery, London.
■ The **Tall Ships Race**, from Torbay to Lisbon, starts with 22 entrants. Twelve are taking part in a special race for vessels over 100 tons. The sailing conditions are tricky – fog and calm.

8 Sunday
New Moon

Brian Kearney (26), a bricklayer from Fort William, sets a new record of 15hrs 2mins for the Three Peaks Climb – Scafell, Ben Nevis and Snowdon. This is 1hr 28mins better than the previous record, set in May.

9 Monday

Torrential rain and thunderstorms in southern England, the Midlands, and East Anglia. In the 2hrs up to 8.30am, London Fire Brigade answers over 300 flood calls. 3 underground stations are shut. *(See panel, facing)*
■ Robert Hance, employed at the UK Atomic Energy Centre, Amersham, is **fined** 10s. after pleading guilty to not stopping at red lights at the junction of Pentonville Road and Penton St. London, on June 6. His defence is that he was driving a lorry with a 2¼ ton radioactive bomb on board, and it would have been dangerous to stop.
■ Fire at the **Maserati** works at Modena, Italy – two cars due to race in the British Grand Prix at Silverstone on Saturday have been damaged and withdrawn from the race. One was Stirling Moss's – he'll now drive one of the three remaining Maseratis.

10 Tuesday

Marcus Kimball, MP for Gainsborough, Lincs, writes to the Director of Education, Lindsey, Lincs, when 250 children are taken ill after eating rissoles prepared at a central kitchen in Gainsborough. The rissoles were made 2 days before they were needed, put in a fridge, then reheated and sent to 15 schools.
■ The House of Lords rejects the **Anti-Hanging Bill**, by 238 votes to 95.

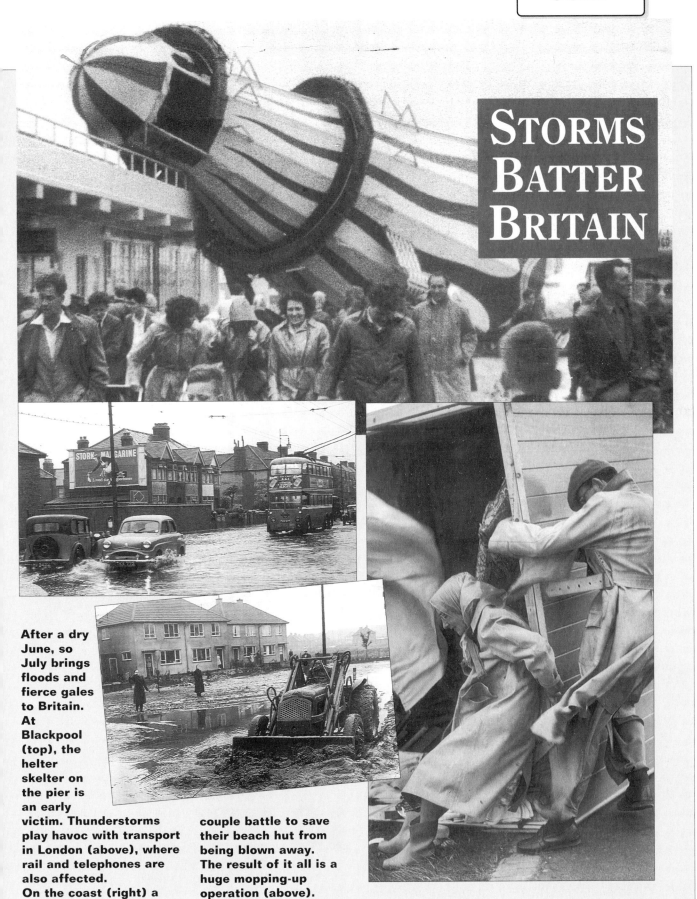

STORMS BATTER BRITAIN

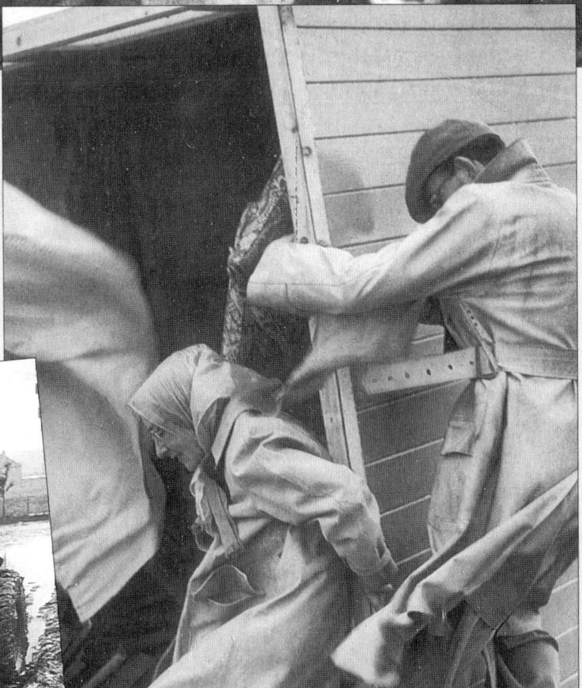

After a dry June, so July brings floods and fierce gales to Britain. At Blackpool (top), the helter skelter on the pier is an early victim. Thunderstorms play havoc with transport in London (above), where rail and telephones are also affected. On the coast (right) a couple battle to save their beach hut from being blown away. The result of it all is a huge mopping-up operation (above).

11 Wednesday

A house being built at Matchams Park Estate, nr Ringwood, Hants, for widow and parish councillor Mrs Elizabeth Mitchell (57) is demolished by Hants Co Council, as it's been built without planning permission. It takes about 20mins to knock it down.

■ The US Air Force airlifts 3,000 needy West Berlin children to West Germany, for summer holidays. Operation Kinderlift is in its third year, and is one of the most popular activities of the Americans in Berlin. The children are chosen by the German Red Cross, which finds them places in private homes for 5 weeks.

12 Thursday

Westfield County Junior School, Woking, Surrey, is closing, with the confirmation of a second case of **polio** in the school. It is the ninth in the area, and two other Woking schools have shut.

■ The first royal **garden party** of the season at Buckingham Palace There are over 8,500 guests including 300 debs from overseas, many in gold and silver-embroidered saris, who have just been presented.

■ Cmdr Nicholas Goodhart and Frank Foster win the world two-seater gliding championship for Britain, with a total of 3828 points over Yugoslavia and Argentina, after a 200-mile race from St Yan, Saone et Loire, France, to St Auban, Jura.

13 Friday

A **summons** against Mrs Elizabeth Marjorie Trevor-Jones (34) is dismissed and she is awarded 7 gns costs, after she was locked in a lodge in Kensington Gardens by park keeper Christopher O'Gorman. The park keeper, said she had been combing a brown dog, and she refused to put the hair in a litter bin when asked. She accused him of being drunk. He walked her from the Broad Walk to the Keepers Lodge at Lancaster Gate, where he locked her in.

■ The 25 ton Argentinian yawl *Juana* is the first boat over the line at Lisbon in the tall ships race, followed by the Turkish yawl *Ruyam*, 102 tons, the first of the larger ships to finish. *Creole*, the stay-sail schooner manned by British cadets, is third.

14 Saturday

■ Argentinian world champion **Juan Fangio**, driving a Maserati, wins the British Grand Prix at Silverstone.

■ A **fire** in the abandoned Wanamaker Department Store, at Broadway and 9th, New York, rages all night before being brought under control. So much water is used that two underground systems are flooded. 400 passengers on 3 trains are rescued with ladders.

. . . All 15 unions involved in BMC's dismissal of 6,000 men approve strike action . . .

15 Sunday

A '**sniper**' in Mornington Crescent, Camden Town, London, damages three buses, but no one is hurt. Police think children with catapults are to blame.

■ Huge crowds in Sydney watch 114 cars start off on the 7,000 mile Ampol **race.** Drivers will go through Canberra, Melbourne, Port Pirie, Alice Springs, Mount Isa, Cairns and Brisbane. The race will last a fortnight, and the winner will get £A3,250 and a cup. Total prize money is £A14,250.

■ There are rumours, emphatically denied, that **Queen Juliana** of the Netherlands, *left*, is contemplating abdication and possibly divorce. It is suggested that the influence of a faith healer is causing a rift between the Queen and Prince Bernhard.

16 Monday

London Bus Week begins with a parade of buses in Regents Park, led by an open-topped, horse-drawn bus. Also on parade is an Ole Bill (1910-1927), driven by George

BSA Boss in Hot Water over Gifts of Furs for His Wife

DATELINE: July 18
SIR BERNARD DOCKER, fighting his dismissal as Chairman and Managing Director of BSA (the Birmingham Small Arms Co), circulates all shareholders saying that claims that he was extravagent are unjustified. The gold Daimler and 4 other cars with special bodywork, which cost BSA £50,000, were for advertising. Sir Bernard says he repaid the company £7,910 for clothes and furs for Lady Docker *(pictured with him).* **BSA say he used a BSA cheque to make the payment. Sir Bernard spends £3,000 on a 3min ITV talk on his battle against his sacking, but it is not broadcast as it does not meet the criteria of impartiality that ITV has to observe.**

Gwynn, who had driven one of more than 1,000 that saw active service in France in World War I.
■ **Diamonds** worth over £100,000 are stolen from a chauffeur-driven Rolls held up at traffic lights in Holborn.
■ **Coloured** people in South Africa who are classified as black will now have to prove that they aren't. Until now, the courts have held it is for the government to prove a person is black, not for the individual to prove he isn't.

17 Tuesday

Governor Earl Long of Louisiana, USA, signs a bill banning interracial athletic contests, dancing, social functions, entertainments and other social contacts between black and white people
■ **Iain Macleod** invites employers and union representatives to talks about the 6,000 men sacked by BMC on June 28. 50,000 men are threatening to strike from next Monday for either reinstatement or compensation. The talks fail.
■ £10,000 reward is offered for information leading to the recovery of the **diamonds** snatched yesterday.

18 Wednesday

Dr Charles Hill, **Postmaster General**, says that each part of the United Kingdom will have its own distinctive stamp. The Queen's head will remain unchanged, but the border will have designs appropriate to each region.
■ British blonde bombshell **Diana Dors** *(right)* signs a Hollywood contract for £50,000 a picture to make 3 films with RKO.
■ **Matyos Rakosi** (65), boss of the Hungarian Communist party, resigns allegedly because of age and ill-health. He is the first of the 'Little Stalins' to go after Khruschev's denunciation of Stalin.

19 Thursday

Lightning strikes one of the last 4 working windmills at Heapham, nr Gainsborough, Lincs. The mill will probably never work again as it is too expensive to repair.
■ **Trans-Siberian railway** services are included in Cook's continental timetable for the first time since 1939. It is now possible to travel to Peking without changing trains at the Manchurian border.

20 Friday

Football League clubs vote 38-10 against accepting an offer from ITV of £110,000 to screen the second half of 35 league matches throughout the season. They also reject the BBC's offer of £67,500 for 12 mid-week evening matches, 20 Saturday games and some FA ties.

21 Saturday

Former RAF fighter pilot J H Denyer, commandant of Newcastle-upon-Tyne airport, wins the **King's Cup**, Britain's premier trophy, in a modified Auster plane at Blackbushe Airport, Hants.

■ The first night of the Proms gets off to a flying start with Elgar's *Cockaine* overture played by the BBC Philharmonic Orchestra conducted by **Sir Malcolm Sargent**.

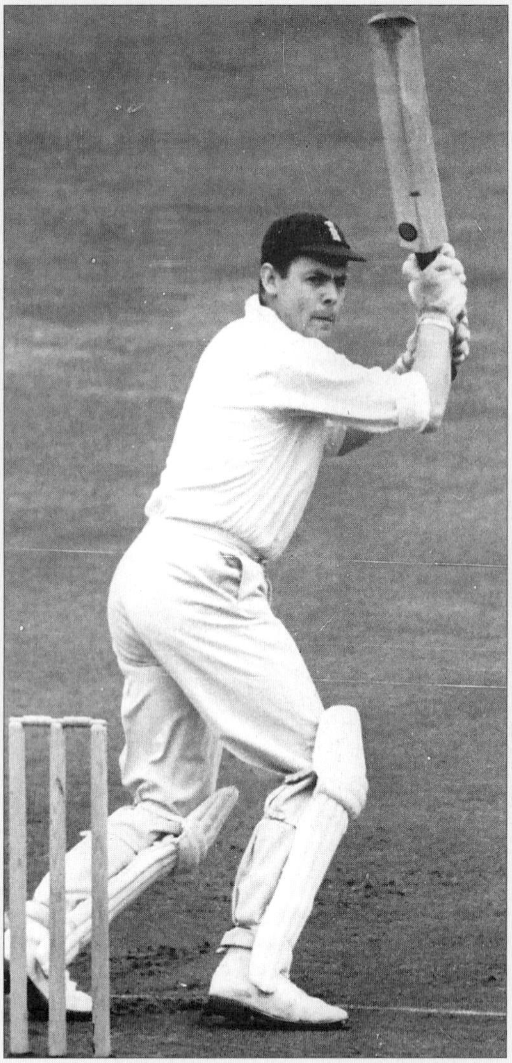

At Last... England in with a Prayer!

Curate DAVID SHEPPARD is called out of the Sunday School class at St Mary's, Islington, by the vicar, who tells him he's been called up for the 4th Ashes Test match against Australia starting at Manchester on Thursday.

22 Sunday

Full Moon

Curate **David Sheppard** is up for the 4th Test Match against Australia *(see panel)*.

■ Wesley Struble (30), takes 9½hrs to **swim handcuffed** across Lake Erie in America. He wears flippers on his feet.

23 Monday

Ford sack 3,000 men from their subsidiary Briggs Motor Bodies in Dagenham. Some of the 15 strike-bound BMC factories supply Ford parts, and they are afraid the strike will still be on when the men return from their annual holiday on August 13.

24 Tuesday

Trouble erupts on the BMC **picket lines** outside the Austin works at Longbridge, Birmingham. Union leaders protest at police interference.

■ Film star **Joan Crawford** (49, *left*) arrives in London with her fourth husband, Pepsi Cola boss **Alfred Steele** (55), and 200 dresses. She has come to make her 73rd film, *Esther Costello*.

■ **Russia** says she will finance Egypt's Aswan High Dam project. Britain and the USA withdrew their offer of finance last week.
. . . Dawn Palethorpe (20) wins the Queen Elizabeth Cup at the International Horse Show at Earl's Court on Earlsrath Rambler. .

25 Wednesday

12,000 **Ford workers** from Briggs Motor Bodies, Dagenham, come out on strike over the 2,000 sacked on July 23. With Briggs at a standstill there will be no Ford bodies to work on and 40,000 workers will have to stop production.
■ **Crane driver** Michael Rankin (30) of North Kensington, saves the lives of 30 of his fellow workers when he falls with the crane when it starts to slip, rather than right the crane by releasing its load on top of them. He survives with a cut arm.
■ American **Bill Steinkraus** beats 25 other riders to take first and second places on *First Boy* and *Night Out* in the King George V Gold Cup at the International Horse Show in London. He decides not to jump off against himself and gives the trophy to the owner of *First Boy*.

26 Thursday

The Italian liner *Andrea Doria* (29,000 tons) collides with the Swedish liner *Stockholm* off Nantucket Island, 90 miles east of New York and sinks. The *Andrea Doria* was equipped with every aid to safety and navigation, but the *Stockholm* has bows specially reinforced for ice breaking.The ship takes 11hrs to sink. 62 people are killed but nearly 2,200 saved, by an armada of ships including the French liner *Ile de France*. The *Stockholm* manages to sail back to New York.
■ A robot called **ERNIE** – Electronic Random Number Indicator Equipment, *(right)* – will select the winning **Premium Bond** numbers. For every £1,000,000 subscribed to Premium Bonds, there will be £40,000 in prizes.

This demonstration model sel
two digits.

■ **Col. Nasser** of Egypt, nationalises the **Suez Canal**. The income will be go to building the Aswan High Dam.

27 Friday

Prime Minister **Sir Anthony Eden** orders a cabinet stand-by in view of Colonel Nasser's nationalisation of the **Suez Canal**. He is thinking of referring the matter to the UN Security Council and freezing the Egyptian government's sterling balances.
■ Film star **Elizabeth Taylor** (25) and her husband (Michael Wilding, *above)* decide to separate.

28 Saturday

British rider Brian Robinson comes in 14th, beating 106 other riders, in the **Tour de France** cycle race which ends in Paris today.
■ The American bowmen of Sherwood, Oregon, USA, win a 'Robin Hood' trans-Atlantic archery match by 9,528 points to 9,447, against the bowmen of Wollaton Park, Notts, 5,000 miles away. They keep in touch by telephone.

29 Sunday

Ninian Sanderson (31) from Glasgow, and Ron Flockhart (32) from Edinburgh win the **Le Mans** 24hr race in a 2yr-old 3.5 litre Jaguar at an average speed of 104.487mph. Jaguar take 6 of the first 8 places.
■ **Col. Nasser** says British ships sailing through the Suez Canal must pay their dues in cash – cheques drawn on British banks are not acceptable. France and the US agree with Britain that the canal must be kept open, by force if necessary. All the services are put on standby.

■ 90mph **storms** rage across Britain, killing 12. It is the worst storm to hit Britain in summer for 50yrs. Lifeboat stations get so many distress calls they have to ask the Navy for help *(see panel, page 59)*.

30 Monday

■ **Col. Nasser**, who yesterday demanded cash for **Suez Canal** dues, now says he'll take cheques payable in London or Cairo.
■ **Dame Edith Evans** (68), who is appearing in *The Chalk Garden*, collapses at home and is admitted to hospital. Actress Gladys Cooper, who is playing the same part in the Brodaway production of the play, flies home to take her place.
. . . Penguin Books is 21 today. The first 10 paperbacks, which were published on July 30, 1935, sold for 6d each . . .

31 Tuesday

Kent **farmers** say that up to 75% of the fruit crop was destroyed by Sunday's gales.
■ £100,000 in East African bank notes disappears from Thomas de la Rue's London printing works. No burglar alarms were triggered, and the thieves left no traces. The loss was discovered during a routine check last Friday.

1 AUGUST

Wednesday

Mrs Doris Thomas (32) and her baby daughter Claudia (17mths) escape with only minor injuries when their **caravan plunges** 200ft over a cliff at Shaldon, Devon. Her husband and two sons were looking for stones to wedge under the wheels.
■ The sacking of **Sir Bernard Docker** is the subject of a 3hr Extraordinary General Meeting of BSA shareholders. Sir Bernard's resolution expressing no confidence in the board is rejected and he accepts dismissal.

USELESS EUSTACE

2 Thursday

France, the USA and Britain call a 24-nation conference to discuss the **Suez Crisis**.
■ **Prince Rainier** of Monaco announces that his wife, **Princess Grace**, is expecting a baby next February. The child will inherit 40 titles. Monaco would lose its independent status and become a French protectorate if the sovereign died without an heir.
■ The BBC signs **Vera Lynn** for a new TV series once a fortnight, starting in October and a new series of *'Yours Sincerely'*, on the Light Programme to begin on August 23.

3 Friday

A Norwegian ship carrying a cargo of Australian wool gets through the **Suez Canal** without paying. She says her tolls were paid in London, where the accounts are frozen. American ships have been told to pay their tolls with a note saying it is under protest and without giving up their rights of possible future recovery.
■ A steward on the liner *Bloemfontein Castle*, on its way to South Africa, is locked in the ship's cells after the Captain receives a message from Scotland Yard that he might know the hiding place of the jewels stolen from Hatton Garden on July 16. The police are on their way to Cape Town.
■ **Willie J. Williams** of Gary, Indiana, breaks Jesse Owens' 20yr-old record for the 100 metres, set in the same stadium in the Berlin Olympics of 1936, with a new time of 10.1sec. Williams will not be running for the USA in the Melbourne Olympics – he couldn't finish the eliminating trials because of cramp.

4 Saturday

Wilhelm Herz of Germany, riding a German NSU 500cc, breaks the **world motorcycling speed record**

Tension Rising over Suez Crisis

EGYPTIAN leader Col Nasser demands that ships using the Suez Canal pay fees to his government. The British and French are firm in their response, sending warships to the area. First, the French Mediterranean fleet is ordered to sail from Toulon. On August 7, the British aircraft carrier *Theseus (right)* sails from Portsmouth for the Mediterranean with men of the 16th Independent Parachute Brigade aboard. Three days later, as tension builds in the area, an airlift of British woman and children home from the Canal Zone begins.

with a speed of 210.64mph over a measured mile at Bonneville Salt Flats, Utah, USA.

■ **Indonesia**, which became independent in 1948, writes off millions of pounds of debts it owes the Netherlands, according to a government statement issued today. The outstanding amount is 4bn Dutch guilders (about £408 million).

5 Sunday

Beryl French (24) of Bournemouth, Hants, wins the women's 8-Day Cycle Race which finishes today in Roanne, France. Six out of the first 10 places are taken by British girls.

■ Derek Emery (6) is rescued by Patrick Harris (11) and Bryan Drewett (15) when he sits on a **live rail** at Sutton, Surrey. Trains are approaching from both directions when the two boys, who are both wearing rubber shoes, pull Derek off the line. Bryan carries him down the embankment, while Patrick dials 999. Derek is badly burned.

6 Monday

Bank Holiday: the coldest for years. Tunbridge Wells, Kent, is hit by a hailstorm and ices up. The ice is up to 3ft deep in some places, and it takes workmen with diggers 4hrs to clear a route for the homeward-bound holiday traffic.

■ John Kelly (39), a deckhand, is taken off the *Bloemfontein Castle* when it arrives in Cape Town, and arrested in connection with the Hatton Garden jewels robbery.

■ The Algerian National Liberation Front orders all **Algerians** living in France to give

SHAME OF RUSSIAN DISCUS STAR

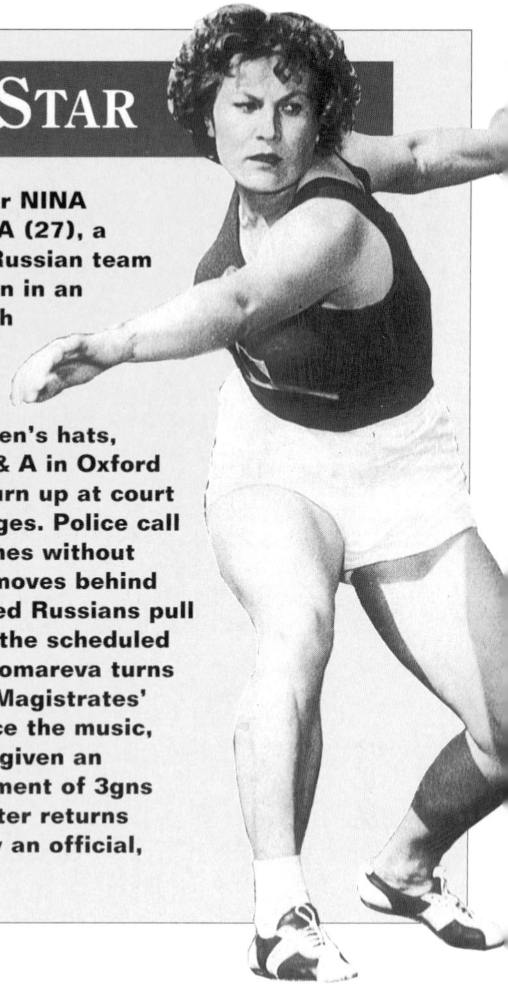

AUG 29

Discus thrower NINA PONOMAREVA (27), a member of a Russian team meeting Britain in an athletics match at White City, is taken to the West End Central police station and accused of stealing 5 women's hats, worth £1.12s.11d. from C & A in Oxford Street. She later fails to turn up at court to answer shoplifting charges. Police call at her hotel, but she vanishes without trace. Despite diplomatic moves behind the scenes, the embarrassed Russians pull out their entire team from the scheduled match against Britain. Ponomareva turns up at Marlborough Street Magistrates' Court on October 12 to face the music, and is found guilty. She is given an absolute discharge on payment of 3gns costs. Miss Ponomareva later returns home *(left)*, accompanied by an official, on the steamship *Molotov*.

up smoking. France has recently increased the tax on tobacco to help fund its fight against Algerian nationalists.

7 Tuesday

London stationers H J Ryman open their first self-service shop at 106 New Bond Street.

■ Professor Armand Delille, who caused **myxomatosis** to spread throughout Europe in 1952 by innoculating rabbits, receives a gold medal as a token of gratitude from the farmers and foresters of France. Millions of rabbits have died as a result of his work.

8 Wednesday

About 250 **miners are trapped** at the Bois du Cazier Colliery, Marcinelle, Belgium after a wagon falls into a ventilating shaft, cutting an electricity cable and causing a short circuit. Fire is raging in two galleries. 139 of the trapped miners are Italian, 115 Belgian and 16 other nationalities, including one Briton. King Baudouin goes to the scene of the disaster.

■ The Italia Shipping Company signs a contract with the Ansaldo Shipyards, Genoa, to build *Andrea Doria II* at a cost of £10 million. The new ship will be able to carry 2,000 passengers, and is due for completion in 1959.

9 Thursday

The Marcinelle **Mine Disaster.** All galleries up to a level of 930ft will be blocked to put out the fires. At least 30 miners have been sacrificed. The rescuers are within 9ft of the lower gallery (2,700ft down) when they have to stop because of excessive heat and no visibility.

■ John Morris, a traveller for a diamond merchant, who has £8,000 worth of **diamonds** in his two cases, watches a smash-and-grab raid in jewellers

B W Francis in Reading, Berks. The thieves get away with rings worth £200.

10 Friday

BOAC offer **emigrants** to the USA and Canada reduced one-way fares (40% below normal tourist rates) to Gander, Montreal, Boston and New York from November to March.

■ The **BMC strike**, which began on July 23, is over. About 2,000 men will get compensation, and BMC will see if any of the 6,000 can be re-employed.

■ A climbing **strawberry** which can grow 6ft high and which produces crops 4-5 times bigger than those of a normal strawberry has been developed by a grower in Holstein, Germany. Called Sonjana, it will be on sale this year.

11 Saturday

Five Manchester boys, given an old sofa for a bonfire, find £3,150 in notes hidden in it. The money belonged to Myer Horowith, a rag dealer, who disappeared in 1939 aged 70, and was presumed dead. It will go to 3 relatives who live locally.

■ D I Thomas Shepherd, who flew to Cape Town to arrest **John Kelly** (see August 6), returns to London with an 18ins cardboard box. He says it is just 'personal belongings.'

. . . The National Trust has acquired Ickworth House, Sussex. The house was accepted by the Treasury in part payment of death duties . . .

12 Sunday

Col. Nasser refuses to attend the Suez Conference in London, and proposes an alternative 45-nation Canal Users' Conference to be held in Cairo. The London Conference will continue with 22 nations attending. Meanwhile, two battalions of the 3rd Infantry Brigade are airlifted to the Mediterranean, and 2 troopships leave Southampton, also bound for the Mediterranean.

■ **Morocco** dismisses 275 French police officers belonging to anti-terrorist brigades and the intelligence services.

13 Monday

There is a national day of **mourning** in Belgium for the victims of the Marcinelle mine disaster.

■ An **oil slick** 2 miles long and 1in deep in places, hits the Solent from Hill Head, Hants to the Hamble River. Holidaymakers are covered in oil and the wind carries it onto cars on the coast road 30yds from the shore. A law banning oil discharges from ships within 100 miles of Britain's coasts comes into effect next month.

■ Labour leaders demand that Parliament is recalled immediately the **Suez Conference** ends so that MPs can discuss the situation.

14 Tuesday

Vauxhall will sack about 1500 workers, rather than the 520 previously announced, because of a further shrinkage in demand for cars and trucks at home and overseas.

■ Actress **Vivien Leigh** (42, *left*), wife of Sir Laurence Olivier, is ordered to take a long rest following the loss of the baby she expected in December.

■ **Col. Nasser** cuts Suez Canal convoys from 4 to 3 a day, 2 southbound and 1 northbound, because of a shortage of pilots. Egypt has been refusing visas to foreign pilots for some time.

15 Wednesday

Playwright **Bertold Brecht** (58) who wrote *The Threepenny Opera, The Rise and Fall of The City of Mahagony, The Resistible Rise of Arturo Ui*, and *The Caucasian Chalk Circle* dies from a heart attack in Berlin.

■ Dr Wharton Young of Howard University

Tough Talking as Suez Crisis Deepens

August sees the stakes increasing in the deadlock over the Suez Canal. When the London Conference on Suez breaks up without agreement, Egyptian leader Col Nasser, *right,* **is asked to meet a five-nation delegation, led by Australian Prime Minister Robert Menzies,** *left,* **Nasser agrees, but digs in, saying he will not accept international control of the Canal, or any plan that affects Egypt's sovereignty over it.**

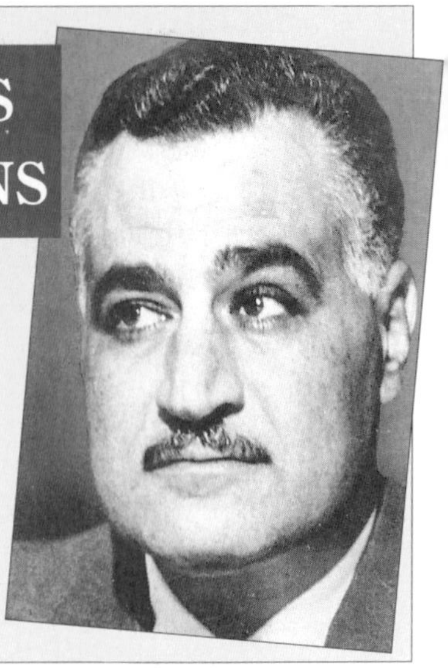

tells the National Medical Association of USA in New York that **baldness** in men is caused by brain growth which squeezes the layer of fat between the skull and the skin, and lessens the blood supply to the hair. Women don't go bald as they have more fat and smaller brains.

■ The mayor of Madrid takes the revolutionary decision to ban the use of **horns** on motor vehicles from today. Madrid has been one of Europe's noisiest cities.

16 Thursday

Leaflets signed by the terrorist leader Dighenis (believed to be Col. George Grivas) are distributed all over **Cyprus** ordering terrorists to observe a ceasefire, to give Archbishop Makarios a chance to solve the Cyprus problem.

■ The government Committee of Public Accounts says the BBC is getting too much money from **licence fees**. The report suggests that all the money should go to the Treasury who would allot the Post Office and BBC sums according to their requirements.

17 Friday

Bert Jackson (80) was determined to have the first pint at a new club in Edenthorpe, Yorks, but he died before it was opened. He'll get his pint, though – the first pint drawn is bottled and Bert's widow, Edith, pours it over his grave in Hatfield Woodhouse cemetery.

■ **Bela Lugosi** (73), star of horror films such as *Dracula,* dies in Hollywood. He went into a mental hospital earlier this year after admitting he'd been a drug addict for 20yrs. He left cured – and penniless.

■ **Adlai Stevenson** wins the nomination as presidential candidate at the Democratic Party Convention in Chicago. Senator **Estes Kefauver** beats Senator John F Kennedy as candidate for the vice-presidency.

18 Saturday

Start of the new **soccer** season.

■ Actor Bela Lugosi is buried in Hollywood, in the black cloak he wore as *Dracula*.

■ The Queen Mother names the new lifeboat at Scrabster harbour nr Thurso, Caithness, *Dunnet Head,* and then goes for a trip in it. The boat, built at a cost of more than £35,000, has been provided by the Civil Service lifeboat fund.

19 Sunday

1,400 miners at the New Stubbin colliery, Rawmarsh, nr Rotherham, Yorks, **strike** for better coal. They are allowed 10 tons of coal a year, at 5s.-9s. a ton. Coal for general sale is screened and washed to take out dirt and stone, but the miners get untreated coal, and they can't burn it.

■ **The Queen** calls a 10-minute Privy Council meeting aboard *Britannia* to approve the wedding of Capt. Alexander Ramsay (36) and the Hon Flora Fraser (25). As Capt. Ramsay's mother, Lady Patricia Ramsay, is the Queen's third cousin, Capt Ramsay has to have the sovereign's permission to marry under the terms of the Royal Marriages Act of 1772.

20 Monday

Fire is still raging at the Marcinelle mine, Belgium, at the 2,509ft level. Efforts to reach the 3,395ft level and recover the bodies of the 168 men still missing have so far failed.
■ A tiny 17ft x 13ft raft, *L'Egare II*, made of cedar logs 2ft thick, with a 4ft cabin in the centre, reaches Falmouth, Cornwall after **drifting** across the Atlantic in the Gulf Stream. It left Halifax, Nova Scotia, in May, with 3 men researching ocean currents for Montreal University on board. It's taken 87 days to reach Falmouth.

21 Tuesday

Full Moon

A 5hr **inquest** in Eastbourne, Sussex, on Mrs Gertrude Joyce Hullett (50), who inherited £94,000 when her husband died last March, reaches a verdict of suicide. The CID are investigating this and the deaths of 12 other rich widows. Mrs Hullett left her doctor, **John Bodkin Adams**, a Rolls Royce, and he had earlier received a cheque for £1,000.
■ Fourteen nations back the British, French and American plan for the **Suez Canal**. They want an International Board to operate, maintain and develop the Canal.

22 Wednesday

Governor of Cyprus **Sir John Harding** offers surrender terms to EOKA terrorists. He gives them 3 weeks from midnight to surrender.
■ **Giacomo La Guardia** (65) of Brooklyn, New York, asks a bell boy for a taxi – but he's on the American liner *United States*, 3hrs out of New York. He had boarded thinking he was going into a hotel. A ship's officer says Mr La Guardia is 'charming but terribly absent-minded'.

23 Thursday

ITV's show '*Spot that Tune*' is seen in 1,048,000 homes – the first time an ITV programme has topped a million since it started last September.
■ Platform 10 at **King's Cross** is closed by police when a lead box falls off a departing express bound for Scotland, and a cylinder containing 15 tiny goldplated radioactive needles falls out. The cylinder is replaced in the lead box by Barbara Brydone (19), who has been rushed up by car from the Government's radio chemical centre at Amersham.

24 Friday

Queen Juliana of the Netherlands has agreed never to see faith healer **Greet Hoffmans** (61, *below*) again, following suggestions (published July 15) of undue influence. A statement by the three eminent men chosen to investigate the rumours, says there is no question of Queen Juliana abdicating, but there will be some changes involving people at court.
■ The ITA has asked the Postmaster General to lift the 6-7pm ban on TV **studio programmes** introduced to allow for bed-

ERSKINE THE NEW BRITISH BOXING HOPE

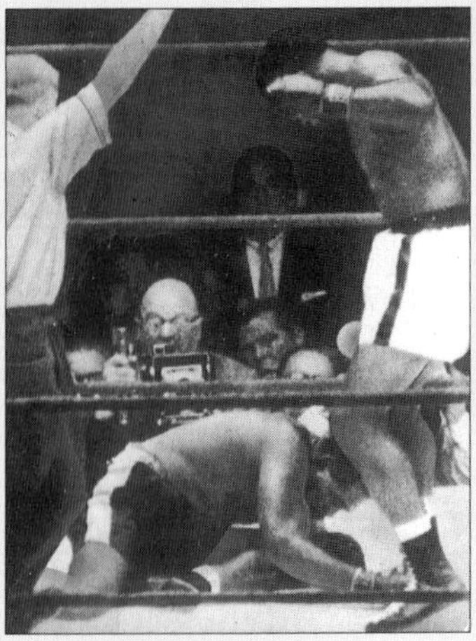

JOE ERSKINE (22, left) becomes domestic boxing's big new hope when he wins the British Heavyweight title on points from Johnny Williams at the Maundy Road Stadium, Cardiff, on August 27. Earlier in the year he claims the Boxing Writers' Young Boxer of the Year award. The year's big fight on the world stage (above) sees Floyd Patterson floor veteran Archie Moore twice in the fifth round at Chicago Stadium to become, at 21, one of the youngest ever world heavyweight champions.

time The BBC oppose the lifting of the ban as it will affect their big radio audiences. *The Archers*, at 6.45pm, has 9 million listeners.

25 Saturday

American architect **Frank Lloyd Wright** (87) is working on plans for a 510 storey office building on the Chicago waterfront. It would be the tallest building in the world (5,280ft). The Empire State building is 102 storeys, 1,472ft high, including the TV mast.

26 Sunday

Sub-Lieut Bernard Commons, of the Royal NZ Navy, has to give up on his 2nd attempt to **swim Lake Windermere** (10½ miles) under water. After 3 miles, water began to seep into his frogman's suit.

■ Colonial Secretary Lennox Boyd says recently captured documents show **Archbishop Makarios** is the actual leader of the EOKA terrorists in Cyprus. He provided money for weapons smuggled from Greece, and was involved in the choice of victims for murder.

■ The **Suez Canal Co** won't accept further responsibility for keeping its pilots working on the Canal as conditions for non-Egyptians are becoming more difficult.

27 Monday

American heiress **Gloria Vanderbilt** (32) marries her third husband TV director **Sidney Lumet** (32), who started life in the slums. *(Picture page 33)*.

■ 3,000 platers, caulkers and burners in a shipyard on the Clyde want to come off piece work and go onto a guaranteed weekly wage, and will strike on Friday unless their demands are met.

■ Troops move into the centre of Nicosia, **Cyprus,** after Col. Grivas threatens more bloodshed unless the British Government start negotiating with Archbishop Makarios.

28 Tuesday

Scotland Yard asks police from Surrey, Hants, Dorset and Yorks to help investigate the mysterious deaths of wealthy women in Eastbourne, Sussex.

■ **Egypt** expels James Gove and John Flux, both first secretaries at the British Embassy in Cairo. They say that James Swinburne, who was arrested for spying on Monday, had 'confessed' to taking orders from them.

29 Wednesday

Russian discus thrower **Nina Ponomareva** is accused of shoplifting *(see panel, page 66).*

■ Britain has agreed to allow France to station troops in **Cyprus**, to ensure the protection of French nationals and their interests in the Mediterranean.

■ Guiseppe Cavallo (23) is charged at Trapani, Sicily, with trying to shoot himself without having a gun licence. **Attempted suicide** is not a crime in Italy.

30 Thursday

Nina Ponomareva, the Russian discuss thrower accused of shoplifting in London, disappears *(see page 66).*

■ 900 welders, members of the Boiler-makers' Society, in 7 shipyards on Tyneside, have voted to **strike** in support of Clyde shipyard workers' fight for a regular wage.

31 Friday

Harry Boon of Cleethorpes (Lincs) gives the Council a daily weather forecast by watching **gnats** on the seashore. For the last month, they've run a competition between Harry and the official Air Ministry weather forecast – result, Harry and the gnats, 127, Met men 123.

■ About 40 small **cinemas** in the Odeon and Gaumont circuits that have been kept open in the hope that would there would be some relief from the entertainment tax in the last Budget, will be closed before the end of October.

■ The **Clyde shipyards** stop work. 3,000 men are sacked. If the strike lasts 10 days, shipyards from Glasgow to Greenock will close, and almost 30,000 men will be idle.

SEPTEMBER

1 Saturday

Italy and Switzerland agree to build a **road tunnel** under the Great St Bernard Pass, linking the two countries. It will be 5.8 km (6,430yds) long.

■ The doors of every church in Hampden, Connecticut, are left open, in case **kidnappers** return baby Cynthia Routolo (6 wks), stolen from her pram. There's been a phone call from a woman saying the baby is safe.

■ The first **boarding schools** in Russia – 285 of them – open at the start of the new school year. The decision to set them up was taken at the Communist Party congress in February, to improve teaching standards and ensure more pupils pass their exams.

2 Sunday

Peter Collins, lying 3rd, and all set to win the World Driver's Championship, gives his car to team-mate **Juan Fangio** (45, *below*) of Argentina when Fangio's car breaks down during the Grand Prix of Europe at Monza, Italy, so that Fangio can become the first man ever to win the championship 4 times.

■ The five-nation **Suez Canal Committee** headed by Australian Prime Minister Robert Menzies arrives in Cairo. Col Nasser says he won't accept international

control of the Canal, or any plan that affects Egypt's sovereignty.
■ **Elvis Presley** sings to 82% of the possible 54 million viewers in the USA on the Ed Sullivan Show.

3 Monday

Rowdy scenes in four London cinemas when *Rock Around the Clock* is shown – 20 youths are taken to court for insulting behaviour.
■ **Marilyn Monroe** has gastritis, and the filming of *The Prince and the Showgirl*, which she's making at Pinewood Studios with **Sir Laurence Olivier,** is replanned so that location shots in which she does not appear can be made.
■ **TUC Congress** opens in Brighton, with 1,001 delegates representing 8,250,000 workers.

4 Tuesday

New Moon

Russia sends pilots from the Baltic to work in the Suez Canal, as talks between the five-nation Suez Canal Committee and Egypt continue. 53 French and 61 British Canal pilots have agreed to stay at work until the talks finish.
■ 300 of 670 boys at Park Lane Secondary Modern school at Tipton, Staffs, are **sent home** on the first day of the new term because of a shortage of teachers.

. . . GORDON PIRIE sets a new world record for the 3,000 metres – 7 mins 52.8 secs at an international athletics match at Malmo, Sweden . . .

5 Wednesday

Gaumont cinemas in S London are not to show *Rock Around the Clock* on Sunday nights, following trouble in N and E London.
■ 'Mind that Child' road safety campaign is launched. Harold Watkinson, the Minister of Transport, calls for better road safety training, especially for child cyclists, and more sense of responsibility from road users toward their own and other people's children.

6 Thursday

Two boys out fishing discover the body of Cynthia Ruotolo, the **baby kidnapped** last Saturday, in a lake 2 miles from Hampden, Connecticut, USA.
■ 210 **National Guardsmen** clear a path for 9 black children to attend a formerly all-white High School at Sturgis, Kentucky, USA, through a rioting mob of miners and farmers. **Tanks escort buses** bringing

BRITAIN ROCKS ARO THE CLOCK WITH BI HALEY & HIS COMETS

A Rock 'n' Roll sensation is sweeping the nation . . . but not without its problems. The film *Rock Around the Clock*, with a title song that is fast becoming an anthem for youth, has the country's youngsters in raptures. Massive queues snake around packed cinema houses, but the music and the message of the film are all but drowned out by some rowdy scenes. The Gaumont chain refuses to show the film in South London on Sunday nights following trouble in other parts of the city. In Manchester, police charge 1,000 screaming, jiving teenagers after the third and last showing of the film at the Gaiety cinema. The film is banned in Stockport and Gloucestershire, and can only be shown with special permission in Ipswich, Taunton and Flintshire.
But it isn't all bad news – the Queen, on holiday at Balmoral, asks to see the film. The royal family were going to see *The Caine Mutiny* . . .

white children to the school. 6 men are arrested.

■ The opening sequence of Hollywood's film version of *Oklahoma!*, starring Gordon MacRae and Shirley Jones, which opens tonight, was shot in Arizona, as they can't grow corn 'as high as an elephant's eye' in Oklahoma.

7 Friday

The five-nation **Suez Canal Committee** talks in Cairo end in complete failure.

■ Pilot the golden labrador (11) is left a £1,000 **trust fund** for life by his late owner, Donald S Appleyard (46) of Roundhay, Leeds.

■ Sportsman **C B** (Charles Burgess) **Fry** (84) dies at his home in Hampstead. He played cricket 18 times for England and as captain never lost a Test against the Australians. He played for Sussex, Hants, and Surrey, scoring 30,406 runs, including 94 centuries. He played in an FA Cup Final for Southampton in 1902, and set the world long jump record in 1892. He also played rugby, was a boxer, golfer, swimmer, sculler, tennis player and javelin thrower. He stood for Parliament unsuccessfully three times.

8 Saturday

The striking miners at Cowpen Mill pit at Blyth, Northumberland, will be back to work on Monday and Jet, the **go-slow pit pony** who caused the strike, will be moved to another job. The 6yr-old pony was so slow hauling tubs of coal that the 'putters' who drove him were losing money.

■ **Stuart Robinson**, an estate agent from Palm Beach, Florida, USA, and the prospective owner of the Kenmare Estate in Ireland, reassures boatmen and jarveys that he will not disturb the Lakes of Killarney. Rowing boats and jaunting cars will not be replaced by motor boats or cars.

9 Sunday

Col. Nasser rejects the 18-nation plan for the international control of the Suez Canal. saying it 'would be not the end but the beginning of trouble'.

■ **Farmers** are facing crippling losses as heavy rain jeopardises the harvest. The land is so waterlogged they can't take machines into the fields.

■ The Swedish ship *Lona* is scuttled in King George's Dock, Hull, to put out a fire that has been raging for 12hrs in her cargo of pit props. Water poured on the ship boils in the heat.

10 Monday

British actress **Jean Simmons** (26), married to film star **Stewart Granger** (42) has a **baby** girl, 7lb 3oz, in Hollywood *(above)*. The baby will be named Tracy, after her godfather, Spencer Tracy.

■ Actor **Leslie Henson** is talking to police enquiring into the deaths of wealthy women in Eastbourne, Sussex, after the sudden death of a close friend in the town some weeks ago. There are 22 names on the police list of suspicious deaths.

■ Two **black children** are driven away by 150 men and women, when they attempt to go into an all-white school at Clay, Kentucky, (pop 1,400).

11 Tuesday

The old **Suez Company** tells non-Egyptian workers, including 61 British and 53 French pilots, they can leave their jobs this weekend. Without them, traffic through the Canal could stop in 10 days.

■ One of the world's richest bachelors, Canadian Dr John Williamson (49) will give **Princess Margaret** a brooch made of 250 stones (worth £15,000) when she visits his diamond mine at Mwadul, Tanganyika, during her East African tour next month.

12 Wednesday

■ A two-day debate on the **Suez Crisis** begins in the Commons, while Egypt says that the American plan to form a Canal Users' Association, discussed only by USA, GB and France, is an act of provocation that could lead to armed aggession and war.

■ The Rank Organisation announce that 39 more **cinemas will close** after Christmas. Added to the 40 shut-downs already announced, this will throw 1,830 out of work.

■ 500 National Guardsmen in full battle kit take over at Clay, Kentucky, where an **armed mob** has been defying the law, so that James Gordon (10) and his sister Theresa can go to school. They spend the day at school amost alone, as most white parents have taken their children away.

13 Thursday

Five mins before end of two-day debate on the Suez crisis, Prime Minister **Sir Anthony Eden** says that except in an emergency he'd refer any situation needing **force** to the UN Security Council.

■ Inventor **A M Low** (68), dies at his home in Chiswick. Called 'the Professor', he had no degree, but he was head of the Royal Flying Corps experimental division and is credited with more than 200 inventions.

. . . It's the WARMEST day in London since July 27. 76ºF in Northolt . . .

14 Friday

The Suez Canal is slowing down, as 90 pilots stop work. 40 Egyptian pilots still at work have been asked to work double shifts.

■ **Farmworkers** serving with the forces will be allowed special unpaid leave to help gather the storm-hit harvest, and the suspension of call-up for farmworkers is extended to December 31.

15 Saturday

Two members of the crew of the *North Britain* (7,189 tons) who decided to go for a swim round the ship, anchored in Cowes Roads, are carried away by the strong tide. One man is rescued, but Seaman Edward Westley (33) of Southampton is feared drowned.

■ Pebbles, the first-ever **King Penguin** chick to be hatched in Canada, and the 2nd on the North American continent, dies in Vancouver of blood poisoning, aged 43 days. Zoo-keepers had tried antibiotic injections without success.

■ **Oliver Hardy** (64, *right*), the fat half of Laurel and Hardy, is seriously ill in a Hollywood hospital after a stroke.

16 Sunday

Yvonne Sugden (16, *below*) British women's ice-skating champion for the last 3yrs, decides to retire.

■ Cargo rates go up to cover for delays through the Suez Canal and rerouting ships round the Cape. Only 6 ships go through the Canal today – the previous average was 41.

■ Muffel the **polar bear** who collapsed at Billy Smart's Circus, Liverpool, on Thursday. opens his eyes for the first time. London Zoo, who were consulted at once, said he needed oxygen, so Muffel's trainer Erich Reichhardt and his assistants have been giving him oxygen 24hrs a day for 3 days and nights.

17 Monday

German-born multi-millionaire **Baron Heinrich Hans von Thyssen** (34) marries his 3rd wife London model Fiona Campbell-Walter (24) at Castagnola, Lugano, Switzerland. One of his four wedding presents to her is a pearl necklace, worth £40,000. *(Picture, page 33)*.

18 Tuesday

Alan McCartney (14) of Low Hill, Wolverhampton, beats RAF experts at RAF station Cosford, Staffs, in a Battle of

Britain **Spot the Plane** competition – most RAF men get 8 or 9 of the10 plane silhouettes flashed on a screen, but he gets the lot.

■ **Prince Michael of Kent** (14, *right*) breaks his wrist running into a wall at Balmoral while playing with Prince Charles. He was in hospital for 5 days in July, after slipping and falling on concrete at Eton College swimming pool.

■ The **average earnings** of all colliery workers during the 2nd quarter of the year were £14.10s. 7d. a week, according to the Coal Board Statistical Review, just published.

19 Wednesday

The **Suez Conference** opens in London. Mr Dulles (USA) appeals for unity in achieving a settlement that is not only peaceful but just.

■ A section of a new bridge across the **Rhine** at Düsseldorf, about 100ft long and weighing about 350 tons, plunges into the river as it is being put into place.

20 Thursday

Full Moon

Harold Watkinson, Minister of Transport, says the growth of road traffic has been completely underestimated, and priority will be given to 5 new motorways. He also says he intends to stop the right of free parking in inner zones of cities.

■ Only 118 bakeries out of 4,200 are open in Paris as **bakers go on strike** – the government won't allow bread prices to rise by 2 francs a kilo, and they can't meet workers' wage claims.

21 Friday

Alexander Wozniak (36) a Polish draughtsman from Dagenham, tries to walk unescorted across the **Channel**, wearing 10ft long canoe-shaped water-skis. About 3 miles from Dover, swift-running tides carry him off course and he's rescued by a passing motor boat.

■ The **Suez Conference** in London ends with a declaration providing for the setting up of a Canal Users' Association. All members of the association will have a seat on its council.

22 Saturday

Carcasses of about 600 animals with **foot-and-mouth** disease have been buried in two of Swindon's water catchment areas at Ogbourne and Wroughton, Wilts. But the Ministry of Health and the Ministry of

CAMPBELL'S RECORD

DATELINE: September 20
DONALD CAMPBELL breaks his own water speed record – from 216 mph to 225.36 mph – in his jet-propelled speedboat *Bluebird* on Coniston Water. On his 1st run over a measured kilometre, he travels at 286 mph.

MARGARET BEWITCHES THE WITCH-DOCTORS!

PRINCESS MARGARET is a popular figure with the locals on her 5-week tour of East Africa. On her arrival in Mombassa, she passes under seven arches of welcome, including one made in the shape of huge elephant tusks. In Zanzibar, she meets Agnes Sudi (nearly 100) and Persis Chimwal (85), who had once been slaves. The Sultana of Zanzibar buys her a hat, costing 3s. 7d. And in Tanganyika, she meets witch-doctors Kitambaa (Bath Mat) and Simba Sultani (King of Lions), left, who perform a 'devil dance' for her.

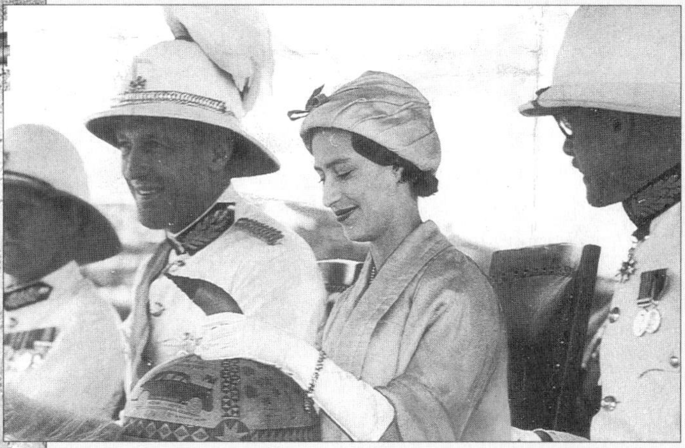

Housing and Local Government say there is no danger of the water being contaminated.

23 Sunday

The burgomaster of **East Berlin** asks West Berlin for the loan of a plaster cast of the quadriga – the bronze statue that used to be on top of the Brandenberg Gate, which was destroyed in the bombardment of 1945 – as they want to restore the gate and replace the quadriga.

■ A **ferry** with about 30 people on board sinks in shallow water at South Beach, Bridlington. As it touches bottom, water comes up to the passengers' necks – they wade ashore, except for a 10yr-old girl, who is carried by fishermen.

24 Monday

The Ministries of Housing, Health, Agriculture and Food decide that no more slaughtered **cattle** will be buried in the Swindon area. Other means of disposal will be found.

■ **Canterbury Cathedral** clock strikes 30 at 9pm, having struck the quarter, half and three-quarters in quick succession at 8pm. It's 101yrs-old, and has been giving trouble since last Friday – one pinion is bent and another is missing.

■ **Hurricane Flossy** storms through the Gulf of Mexico towards the coastline of Alabama and Florida with winds of up to 100mph. There's torrential rainfall in the Mississippi delta, and 3 die.

25 Tuesday

Wladziu Valentino **Liberace** *(above)*, the American pianist, is welcomed by a crowd of over 3,000 when he arrives in at Waterloo station in London.

■ The **transatlantic telephone** cable linking Britain and America between Oban, Scotland, and Clarenville, Newfoundland – the longest submarine telephone system in the world – is completed two months ahead of schedule.

■ **Hurricane Flossy** drives 10,000 from their homes in the flooded Mississippi Delta, then turns east to Alabama and Georgia.

■ A 500ft steel mast used to transmit BBC Home Service to London and SE is **wrecked** when it collapses into a field at Brookmans Park, Herts.

26 Wednesday

The **UN Security Council** will debate the Suez Canal dispute next week.

■ Uganda, with a team playing mostly in bare feet, beat the British **Olympic football** team 2-1 at Ilford.

■ Pasteurised milk is sometimes 60hrs old and solid in the bottles when it arrives on village doorsteps, the council meeting of Oxfordshire WIs is told. They say the old unhygienic days when the milkman put milk straight into jugs were better.

27 Thursday

The Rootes Group are discussing with the unions the probable **dismissal** of 500 workers at two Coventry factories, mostly because of overseas shipping difficulties.

■ The Peak Park Planning Board announces plans to open more large areas of Derbyshire moors to walkers, including Kinder plateau, Edale, Bleaklow plateau and Hallam moor.

28 Friday

Liverpool's overhead railway will cease operating on December 30. A proposal to turn the track into an overhead motorway wins no support.

■ Dr Deborah Coggins, the only woman county health officer in Florida, is to be dismissed for having lunch with a **black nurse** in a restaurant.

■ After examining Javier Pereira of Columbia for 9 days, doctors at the New York Hospital – Cornell Medical Centre say he's very old and possibly more than 150. Mr Pereira says he's 167 – which makes him the **oldest man** in the world.

29 Saturday

Clement Davies (72) resigns as leader of the Liberal Party at the end of the party conference at Folkestone. He's been leader since 1945.

■ A proposal to abolish the huff is brought up at the annual meeting of the British **Draughts** Association. A ballot of all 500 members will be held to settle the point.

■ Hundreds of people attend ceremonies recalling the landing of Sir Francis Drake in California on June 15, 1579. He claimed the area – calling it New Albion – for Queen Elizabeth I.

30 Sunday

Aircraft mechanic Thomas Fitzpatrick lands a light plane between rows of apartment houses on St Nicholas Avenue, Manhattan, New York, at 3am. He tells police he has engine trouble.

■ Residents of Northern Queensland are

Vulcan Bomber in Crash at Heathrow

DATELINE: October 1. An RAF VULCAN delta-wing bomber crashes in flames at London airport, in full view of waiting relatives and high-ranking officers, after a 26,000 mile return flight to Australia and New Zealand. The pilot and co-pilot use their ejector seats and survive; the remaining crew of four are killed.

testing sudden unexpected heavy rain to see if it's radioactive. Since the atomic explosion at Maralinga, S Australia, a cloud of radioactive dust has drifted N E across the continent. Every town in its path has had sudden rainfall, including parts of Queensland that have been dry for 8mths.

■ Hitler's designated successor, Karl Dönitz, is released from Spandau prison in Berlin after completing the 10-year sentence imposed on him at Nuremberg.

OCTOBER

1 Monday

The oldest living things in the world have been discovered by scientists at Arizona University – three bristlecone pine trees, thought to be more than 4,000yrs old, growing at an altitude of about 10,000 ft in the White Mountains, nr Bishop, California.

■ The start of a fortnight's celebration for Tokyo's 500th birthday.

2 Tuesday

A dynamometer, costing well over £100,000 and the only one in Britain, is installed by the Dunlop Rubber Co in their Coventry works. It can test aircraft wheels, brakes and tyres simultaneously, and can reproduce almost any operating conditions.

■ Mrs Jessie Williamson, a **botanist** and plant collector, has discovered a plant new to science in the Misuku foothills nr Karonga, Rhodesia. It's about 1ft high and has greenish-yellow flowers about 3in long. It has been named *Ceropegia mirabilis*.

3 Wednesday

Great Yarmouth Council, Norfolk, want to stop people eating fish and chips on buses after a conductor is injured when he slips on a chip on the stairs and falls.

■ People in Fraserburgh, Aberdeenshire, are so **angry** that British Railways don't plan to decorate the station on Saturday when the Queen Mother and the Queen of Denmark come to the wedding of Flora Fraser to Capt Alexander Ramsay, that BR give in.

4 Thursday

New Moon

Governor Sir John Lavarack declares a **State of Emergency** throughout Queensland, Australia, in a dramatic move to end the 9-month-old sheepshearers' strike. The strikers are ordered to return to work by October 8 or face a maximum fine of £A100.

■ Two female cygnets hatched in the lakes nr Grand Prairie, Alberta, Canada, are on their way to England by plane as a gift for the Severn Wildfowl Sanctuary. They will replace two rare trumpeter swans given to the Queen and Duke of Edinburgh in 1951, which died.

... SNOW falls as far south as the Lake District and Pennines ..

5 Friday

UN Security Council meets to discuss the Suez crisis.

■ Cesspit cleaner Herr Koelsch of Siegen is allowed by a Cologne court to use his **telephone** number, 4711, for ordinary business purposes, but not for advertising *(see July 8)*.

IT'S MY WORLD!

DATELINE: October 15
Student Petra Schurmann (23), Miss Germany, wins the Miss World title in London, earning £500 and a sports car. Miss USA (Betty Cherry of North Carolina) is 2nd, Miss Israel (Rina Weiss) is 3rd.

■ The National Trust will prosecute people who drop litter in their properties. 2½ tons of **litter** was collected on Box Hill after August Bank Holiday.

■ Hundreds of people stand knee-deep in water, with many more packed onto roofs and in trees, to greet **Princess Margaret** when she arrives in Zanzibar. *(See panel, page 77).*

6 Saturday

A pontoon bridge joins the **Isle of Sheppey**, Kent, to the mainland again. Sheppey has been marooned since the Kingsferry Bridge, the only road and rail link, was put out of action on Friday by a Norwegian steamer.

■ A **vaccine** that can be taken by mouth and will give long-term, maybe life-long, protection against all 3 major strains of **polio** is announced by Dr A B Sabin of the University of Cincinnati, USA.

7 Sunday

Monkeys, a kangaroo and performing dogs are let loose when fire breaks out in a generator van between Thorne and Keadby Bridge, Yorks, belonging to Fossett's Circus.

■ **Princess Margaret** is given a golden dhow by the people of Pemba Island, Zanzibar.

8 Monday

Fifty prominent people, including union leaders, bankers, and diplomats urge Britain to join the 6 nations drafting a European

common market treaty, instead of just 'associating' with it as the government plans.
■ Police dog Rex III (6½), an Alsatian, dies of throat cancer. The most outstanding police dog of the year last year, he demonstrated tracking to royalty, made many arrests, and starred in the film *Police Dog*.
■ **Clarence Birdseye** (69), inventor of frozen food, dies in New York after a heart attack.
■ Shellmex, BP and Power Petroleum announce that **petrol** will go up by ½d. a gallon from tomorrow morning.

9 Tuesday

For 2yrs gardener Aubrey Smith has nurtured a banana palm at Swansea's botanic gardens, but today, just before the first bunch of bananas are ripe, they are stolen.
■ Police Sergeant Norman Loxley of Isleworth and PC Thomas Oliver of Hanworth, *right*, are awarded the **George Cross**. Ignoring the live rail, they fought their way into a blazing electric train at Barnes, Surrey, last December, and rescued a man trapped under the wreckage. 13 people died.

10 Wednesday

Tory Party Conference begins at Llandudno.
■ Mrs Daphne Case catches a 7ft 8in blue shark weighing 134lbs off Looe, Cornwall, and claims the women's world fishing record.
■ **Balloonist** Charles Dollfuss takes his hydrogen gas-filled balloon into the new church at Yvetot, nr Rouen, France, to help workmen painting the 75ft high ceiling.
■ At least five people are killed and 100 injured during riots in Kowloon, Hong Kong – the riots begin when anti-Communist refugees from the Chinese mainland begin to stage Nationalist Day demonstrations.

11 Thursday

A freak blast from Britain's 8th **atom bomb** test at Maralinga, South Australia, causes a tremendous double explosion at Kingoonya, nr Adelaide, over 200 miles away. Children run screaming from school in terror at the noise and shaking.
■ A taxi is **attacked** by the mob and set on fire in the second day of continuous rioting in Hong Kong.The driver burns to death: the passenger, Swiss consul Fritz Ernst, drags his badly-burned wife from the wreckage and fights off the mob until help arrives.

12 Friday

After a secret 2hr session of the **UN Security Council** in New York, Egypt agrees to six points put forward by Britain's Foreign Secretary **Selwyn Lloyd**, which include free and open transit through the Canal without discrimination, and respect for Egyptian sovereignty, and will form the basis of future negotiations.
■ **Nina Ponomareva** (27) boards Soviet liner *Vyacheslav Molotov* on her way home. after being found guilty of shoplifting in London *(see page 66)*.

13 Saturday

The first **new museum** to be built in Britain since the war is opened in Stoke on Trent. The museum has very fine pottery exhibits, from Romano-British to the present day.
■ Senior Commissioned Boatswain George Wookey (34) of Portsmouth, a diver for

12 yrs, sets a new world record for deep diving with a descent of 600ft from HMS *Reclaim*, the Navy's experimental diving ship, in Norwegian waters.

14 Sunday

Southdown bus company, Hants, is trying to identify the **conductor** who turned Ronald Catcheside (8) off the bus at Hilsea, leaving him to walk home seven miles with a case of school books. He had lost his pass.

■ Settlers spot four **Egyptian commandos** about to attack Israeli Prime Minister David Ben Gurion's home in the Negev Desert. Two are shot and two wounded and captured.

15 Monday

■ **Marilyn Monroe** is sent a fan letter more than 20ft long by 200 knitwear workers from Hawick, Roxburghshire. Last week they sent her a cashmere sweater.

■ The **Duke of Edinburgh** leaves London Airport at the start of a 35,000 mile world tour. He'll join the royal yacht *Britannia* in Mombasa, and go on to Melbourne to open the Olympic Games on November 22.

16 Tuesday

Cranedriver Charlie Monnery scoops up a live half-hundredweight shell in a load of ballast he is shifting from a ship at Shoreham, Sussex. His mate, Bert Huntley, lifts the shell out, and an Army bomb-disposal squad makes it safe.

■ A **crippled** PanAm plane on a flight from Honolulu to San Francisco with 31 people on board circles a weather ship 1,000 miles out in the Pacific for 3hrs before landing on the sea and breaking into two. All 24 passengers and seven crew are rescued.

■ **Princess Margaret** meets the District Commissioner for Masailand, Francis Townsend (31), at a tribal gathering at Arusha, Tanganyika He is the brother of Peter Townsend, whom she decided not to marry last year. The brothers look very alike.

17 Wednesday

Actor **Bernard Miles** is formally given the lease of land at Puddle Dock by the Lord Mayor of London for building the *Mermaid Theatre* – the first theatre ever in the city.

■ The Queen opens the world's first commercial **atomic power station** at Calder Hall on the Cumberland coast. With the flick of a switch she sends atomic-powered electricity into the homes of 20,000 people.

■ The biggest hit at the motor show, which opens today, is the smallest car, the **Berkeley** two-seater sports car *(left)*. It does 70mph, 50 miles to the gallon and costs £575 including purchase tax. The company has been flooded with orders.

18 Thursday

Mrs Mary Hunter (27) formerly of Ewell, Surrey, her husband Gerry Hunter (34), employed by the Canadian Fisheries Service, and George Gonzales, an Argentinian-born pilot, are rescued by a Royal Canadian Air Force plane fitted with skis, which lands on a frozen lake 129 miles N of Yellowknife in the NW Territories, Canada. They've been missing, thought dead, since September 29. Today second pilot Richard Warner, frost-bitten and exhausted, staggers into a mining camp – it has taken him seven days to cross 28 miles of frozen swamp.

19 Friday
Full Moon

BBC and ITV sign an **agreement** by which each will be able to make newsreel films of sporting events to which the other has exclusive 'live' rights.

■ **Elvis Presley** (21), is cleared of the charge of assault and battery by a court in Memphis, Tennessee, after a fight with two men at a petrol station on Thursday. Garage man Ed Hopper (42) became angry when

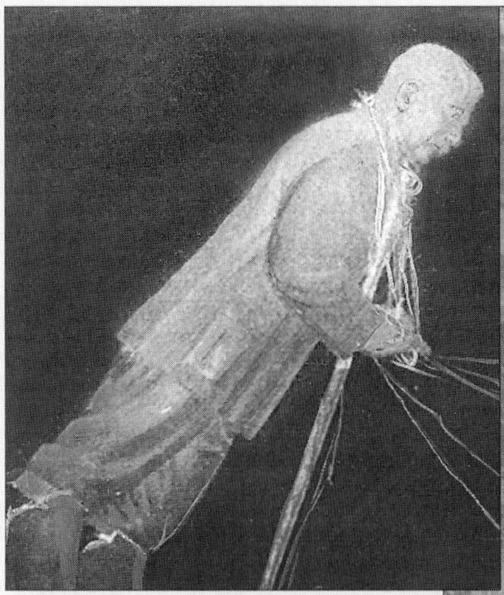

Russian Tanks Roll in to Quell Huge Uprising in Hungary

In the last week of Ocotber, the people of Hungary rise in revolt against the Communists. Casualties are heavy as ordinary people attack Russian tanks with their bare hands, though as Hungarian troops join the revolt the rebels begin to acquire weapons. On November 5 at dawn, 1,000 Soviet tanks roll into Budapest and, by lunchtime, Moscow Radio claims that the revolt has been crushed. One percent of Hungary's population become refugees. *Top left:* **A huge bronze statue of the hated Stalin is toppled.** *Middle left:* **Russian tanks in the heart of Budapest.** *Bottom left:* **Hunger in Hungary.**
Below: **A Russian armoured car destroyed by rebels.** *Bottom:* **Rebels march on Lenin Ring. Paving stones are torn up and used as weapons.**

fans surrounded Presley's car. He threatened the singer with a knife but Presley, who boxed as an amateur, fought back.

20 Saturday

The French liner *Ile de France* arrives safely in Le Havre following the worst storm she's ever met in the Atlantic.

■ Australian **Lorraine Crapp** (18) breaks all four of her own world swimming records for the 200m, the 220yd, the 400m and 440yds at an Olympic carnival in Sydney. She's the first woman to beat 5min for the 440yd freestyle in a time of 4min 48.6 sec.

■ **Jean Seburg** (17, *left*) a chemist's daughter from Marshalltown, Iowa, USA, is chosen by Otto Preminger from 18,000 hopefuls to play *St Joan* in his new film of Shaw's play.

■ **Burnley's** record of 30 League games without defeat still stands after Manchester United, within four games of the total, lose 2-5 to Everton.

21 Sunday

Poland's Communist leaders sack Russia's **Marshal Rokossovsky** from his post in the Politburo, and elect Wladyslaw Gomulka (51), who wants to free Poland from Russian control, as Secretary General of the Polish Communist Party.

■ **Princess Margaret** phones the Queen from Government House, Nairobi, Kenya, to say that Mau Mau boss Dedan Kimathi has been captured. Police have been hunting for him for weeks.

22 Monday

Admiral Earl Mountbatten (56) First Sea Lord *(right)*, is promoted to Admiral of the Fleet – achieving his lifelong ambition to attain the same rank and position as his father, Prince Louis of Battenberg.

■ Russia sends two **cruisers** into Polish waters, saying they're on manoeuvres.

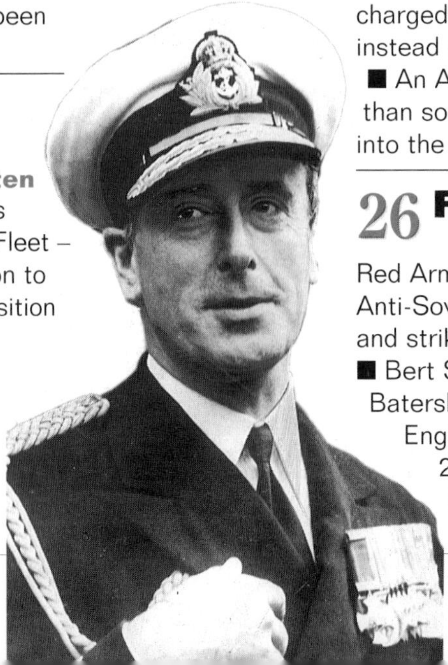

■ Greece asks for self-government for Cyprus within the Commonwealth.

23 Tuesday

Mrs Mary Green, who emigrated from England with her 11 children under the assisted passage scheme five months ago, stows away with 10 of them on the luxury liner *Orsova* in Melbourne. When they are discovered, the crew offer to send the **unhappy** family back to Britain, but Mrs Green has first to reimburse the Australian government for their fares out.

■ 200,000 members of the Hungarian Youth Organisation march on the parliament building in **Budapest**, demanding the restoration of ex-Premier Imre Nagy and the return of the Red Army to Russia.

24 Wednesday

Fighting between anti-Russian rebels and Red Army troops rages in **Budapest** *(see page 83)*.

■ The Post Office have decided to give people 12 more days to pay their phone bills before cutting them off. Subscribers have previously had 31 days to pay.

25 Thursday

More Russian tanks and troops move into **Budapest**. Estimates of the death toll range from 200 to 2,000.

■ From December 1, NHS patients will be charged for every item on a **prescription**, instead of 1s. per prescription.

■ An American Navy jet fighter flying faster than sound **shoots itself** down by flying into the shells it fired seconds before.

26 Friday

Red Army tanks pour into **Budapest**. Anti-Soviet radio stations broadcast battle and strike orders *(see page 83)*.

■ Bert Smith (31) of Toronto and Alan Batersby (29) of Blackpool are nearing England after crossing the Atlantic in a 26ft home-made ketch *Orenda*. They left Canada 56 days ago.

27 Saturday

Premier **Imre Nagy** *(right)* orders Russian troops out of Budapest *(see page 83)*.
■ **Princess Margaret** watches Galina Ulanova and the Bolshoi Ballet in *Romeo and Juliet* at Covent Garden.

■ All Russian tanks leave **Budapest** on the 9th day of bitter fighting. The rebels have released political prisoners, including **Cardinal Mindszenty**, head of the Roman Catholic church in Hungary who was gaoled in 1949 for 'treason'.

28 Sunday

Imre Nagy broadcasts a peace offer after insurgents threaten to march on **Budapest.** Hungary withdraws from the Olympic Games because of the disturbances.

29 Monday

Israeli tanks and armoured cars over-run the Egyptian border and thrust 70 miles towards the **Suez Canal**. They claim to be only 18 miles from the Canal.
■ Marilyn Monroe, Brigitte Bardot, and Anita Ekberg are among the stars lining up to meet the Queen and Princess Margaret at the Royal Film performance. The film is *The Battle of the River Plate*.
■ After a change of heart, **Hungary** will now compete in the Olympic Games.

30 Tuesday

Egypt rejects and Israel accepts a 12hr **ultimatum** which asks Egypt to allow Anglo-French troops to move temporarily into the Canal Zone, and orders Egyptian and Israeli forces to withdraw 10 miles on both sides of the Canal. If a reply isn't received Anglo-French troops will intervene.
■ As **frost** damage last winter affected 18 out of every 100 council houses, the government is preparing a short TV film to show people simple precautions.

31 Wednesday

No reply to their **ultimatum** has been received so British and French forces begin an air and navy bombardment of Egyptian military targets.

NOVEMBER

1 Thursday

Allied navies close in on both ends of the **Suez Canal**.
■ Premium Bonds go on sale – Mayors throughout the country buy them, but not the Lord Provost of Glasgow, Andrew Hood – he doesn't approve of gambling.
■ Premier **Imre Nagy** says that Hungary is now independent, and appeals to the UN and the 'great powers' to help in preserving the country's neutrality. Russian tanks ring Budapest.

2 Friday

New Moon

The Admiralty broadcasts warnings to merchant ships to keep clear of both ends of the **Suez Canal** – invasion fleets are thought to be stationed there. Egypt blocks the canal by sinking 95 ships. The government appeals to the public to cut back on oil consumption.
■ Russian air and land forces move into **Hungary** in strength with more than 600 tanks, heavy bombers and fighters. The roads from Budapest to the Austrian border are sealed. The UN debates the situation.
■ The **Olympic flame** is lit by Greek girls at Olympia, and handed to the first of 3,100 runners who will carry it by relay to Melbourne.

3 Saturday

A convoy of British trying to leave **Egypt** reach Alexandria, but are turned away as they have no exit visas.
■ Anthony Nutting, Minister of State at the

Foreign Office, **resigns** from the government over Suez. The Prime Minister broadcasts to the nation on the Crisis.

■ Fifty-nine of 133 **miners trapped** in a coal mine at Springhill, Nova Scotia, Canada, are found alive more than a mile below ground, after an explosion yesterday. 13 die.

4 Sunday

There are 213 starters in the London – Brighton **veteran car** run. 204 complete the 51-mile journey.

■ In London, a crowd of 10,000 clash with 500 police in Whitehall as they **demand** Sir Anthony Eden's resignation and the end of the war with Egypt.

5 Monday

Allied forces gain control of **Port Said** after heavy fighting. A cease-fire is accepted by Egypt, Israel, Britain and France.

■ 1,000 Soviet tanks and 10 Soviet divisions attack **Budapest** at dawn to crush Hungarian resistance. The Nagy government is overthrown.

■ The Royal Variety Show is cancelled a few hours before it is due to start because of the international situation.

■ **Jo Grimond** is elected the new leader of the Liberal Party.

■ A Hermes transport with 54 people on board crashes and bursts into flames at Blackbushe Airport, Hants. It had taken off from Tripoli, bringing home 34 service families from the Middle East.

6 Tuesday

Dwight D Eisenhower has a runaway success in the US Presidential election.

■ British troops have ceased fire in **Egypt**, but Cairo radio says Egyptians will fight on as long as there are aggressors on Egypt's soil. The Allied forces hold most of a 47-mile stretch of the canal between Port Said and Ismailia.

■ **The Queen** opens Parliament. The Government will rush through a Bill giving landlords of five million privately-owned rent-controlled houses the power to raise rents.

SUEZ CRISIS TAKE

BRITAIN TO THE BRINK OF WAR

Vhen Col. Nasser nationalises the Suez Canal, the ital lifeline for oil supplies to Europe and still egally the property of the Anglo-French Suez Canal Company, confrontation is inevitable. The outbreak of fighting between Israel and Egypt triggers Franco-British 'intervention', and allied forces seize control of the Canal Zone. But the overwhelming disapproval of the US government, convinced there is a collusion between Israel, France and Britain, and the crushing inancial pressure they exert, backed by the condemnation of the United Nations, persuades rance and Britain to pull out their forces. *Pictures, clockwise from top left:* Prime Minister Eden is hanged in effigy beneath a portrait of Col. Nasser in Port Said; blazing oil tanks blot out the sky in Port Said; Sunken ships block the canal entrance; The window of Port Said lighthouse, riddled with bullet holes after the fighting; an anxious crowd awaits the outcome of the emergency Commons debate; A British soldier watches the arrival of the UN contingent.

■ The Dockers' luxury yacht *Shemara,* 870 tons, is up for sale, price £500,000. It's 18yrs old, and was an anti-submarine training ship in the war.

7 Wednesday

America supports the UN resolution ordering Britain, France and Israel to quit **Suez.** Prime Minister Sir Anthony Eden has already told the Commons that Britain won't leave Egypt until the UN takes over.

■ Garages' **petrol** and oil supplies are being cut by 10% – drivers rush to fill up.

8 Thursday

Many countries withdraw from the **Olympics**. There will be no teams from Egypt, Communist China, Iraq, Holland, and Spain. Switzerland and Norway are considering withdrawal.

■ The puppet Hungarian government set up by the Russians starts threatening people with **reprisals** if they don't get back to work, but fierce fighting continues. Refugees stream into Austria.

PETROL RATIONING IS HERE

The Suez Crisis brings with it petrol shortages. After an initial cut in supplies of 10%, the shortfall becomes so severe that rationing is introduced, on December 17, and driving tests cancelled, except for the disabled. Motorists are allowed petrol for 200 miles a month. Post Offices issue ration books.

9 Friday

The London-Edinburgh express is stopped by police at New Barnet, 19mins out of King's Cross, when a phone call warns there is a bomb on board. The 230 passengers get off, and police search the train, but nothing's found.

■ UN tells Russia to quit **Hungary**, where the danger of starvation, widespread epidemics and disease is increasing. The **Red Cross** manages to get through with coal and wood.

10 Saturday

Villagers get **free coal** at Winlaton, Co. Durham, after workmen making a road find a coal seam. It's too small to interest the Coal Board, so the council says villagers can have the coal, as the site must be cleared.

■ The Swiss Foreign Minister says that 450 British workers maintaining installations on the **Suez Canal** have been interned.

11 Sunday

Advance units of the UN police force assemble in Italy, but Egypt has not yet agreed to allow them in.

■ The Hungarian relief fund has passed £50,000 mark. Meanwhile, Hungary's Olympic team arrives in **Melbourne**. They won't fly the Communist flag outside their quarters, but the old red, white and green flag of Kossuth's freedom movement.

12 Monday

100 Sidney Street, Stepney, where police and troops directed by the Home Secretary, Winston Churchill, besieged **Peter the Painter** and another criminal in 1911, is pulled down to make way for flats.

■ The bill for the **Suez** campaign is between £35m and £45m, says the Minister of Supply, **Reggie Maudling**.

■ Ex-Queen **Elizabeth of Greece** (62, *left*), dies of heart disease at Cannes. She was the divorced wife of George II of Greece and a great-granddaughter of Queen Victoria.

■ All boys over eight, old enough to carry weapons, are being rounded up and deported from Hungary to Russia by secret police.

13 Tuesday

Reports from Vienna say that 200 Hungarian miners at the Tatavanya coalfield have been deliberately **entombed** by the Russians. The miners had run out of ammunition and taken refuge in the pit: the Russians blew in the pithead.

■ The Medical Research Council's **anti-smog** team of six doctors and scientists is in action for the first time this winter, trying out new masks at St Bartholomew's Hospital, when fog blankets London and the Home Counties.

■ Film star **Ingrid Bergman** (39) has her appendix out in hospital in Paris.

14 Wednesday

Prince Charles' birthday – he is 8 today.

■ UN troops are ordered into **Egypt** by Secretary General Dag Hammarskjøld, after news from Moscow that President Nasser has asked for Russian 'volunteers' to help against Anglo-French troops.

■ Within hours of her lawyer filing papers for divorce from **Michael Wilding** in Santa Monica, California, film star **Elizabeth Taylor** (25) and film producer **Michael Todd** (49) leave New York for a fishing holiday in Miami, Florida.

15 Thursday

French police are looking for the perpetrator of the 10th trunk murder in 8yrs, after finding the mutilated body of a man in a trunk nr Grenoble.

16 Friday

The first Hungarian **refugees** fly into London including a 26yr-old mother who pushed her 18-month-old daughter 40 miles in a pram.

■ A joint Franco-British salvage company is formed in Port Said to clear the **Suez Canal** of the 47 ships and two bridges that have been sunk in it.

17 Saturday

No petrol will be on sale in France at weekends: garages must close from noon Saturday to noon Monday.

■ A plaque commemorating the knighting by **King James I** of a loin of beef (Sir loin) at Hoghton Tower, Lancs, and presented by the National Beef Council of America, is unveiled at the Tower by Sir Cuthbert de Hoghton.

18 Sunday

Full Moon

The search by 70 police and 1,200 volunteers for Boyd Fearon (3), of Romford, Essex, missing since last Thursday, is called off.

■ Mrs Ellen Moore, of Wallsend, has a 7lb 12oz boy at Newcastle Hospital on her 23rd birthday. She was unconscious for 169 days after receiving head injuries in a road accident on May 4. They used cooling anasthesia to keep her in a state of hibernation.

19 Monday

Hull dockers refuse to load the *Balashov*, the first Russian ship to reach Hull since the uprising in Hungary.

■ John Kelly (37), arrested on the

Bloemfontein Castle on August 6, and three other men are found guilty of stealing diamonds worth £75,000 from a Rolls-Royce in Farringdon Road on July 16. Kelly gets three years.

■ **Sir Anthony Eden** cancels his public engagements. His doctors say he's suffering from severe overstrain.

20 Tuesday

The British Red Cross relief fund for **Hungary** has reached £159,000. It will provide a convoy of 15 vehicles three times a week for a month.

■ **Petrol rationing** will start on December 17 (see page 89).

21 Wednesday

About 600 gallons of petrol seeping from a city-centre garage leaks into the drains, telephone and electricity networks at Peterborough, Northants. Firemen, post office and electricity workers try to prevent an explosion.

■ 7,000 Hungarian refugees crossed into Austria yesterday . . .

22 Thursday

Lord Mayor of London Sir Cullum Welch hands over £108,000 to 6 relief organisations for Hungarian refugees. His appeal has raised £405,000 in 10 days.

■ The **Duke of Edinburgh** opens the Olympic Games in Melbourne. The Hungarians, some of whom don't have their uniforms, receive an emotional reception.

■ Austria appeals for **aid** for 60,000 refugees – 8,410 have arrived in the last 24hrs. Britain has taken 579.

23 Friday

Former premier of Hungary **Imre Nagy**, and 40 companions, who left the shelter of the Yugoslav Embassy in Budapest yesterday appear to have been **abducted** to Rumania.

■ Twenty-seven children aged 2-7 are carried to safety when **fire** breaks out in a kindergarten in Brighton, Sussex.

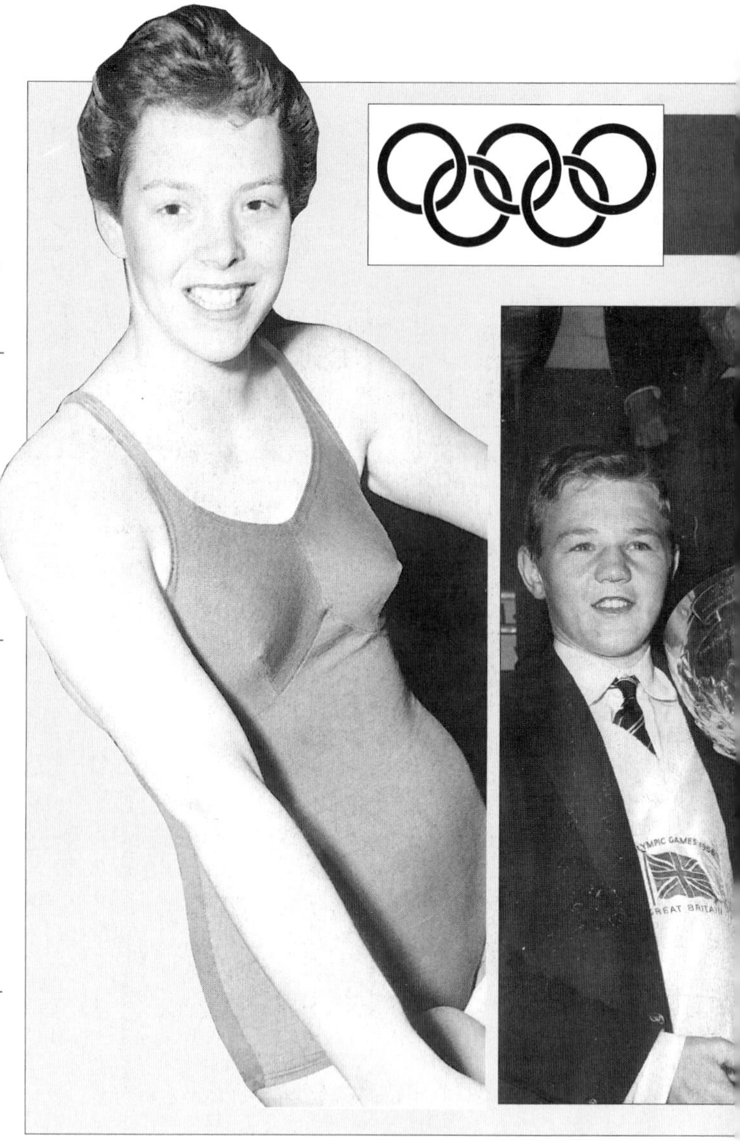

■ An Italian plane on its way from Rome to New York crashes in flames on a house at Orly, Paris, shortly after take-off, killing 33 of the 34 people on board.

24 Saturday

Alan Crompton (28) of Hale, Cheshire, captain of the Olympic ski team, travels 240 miles on water-skis on Lake Windermere, in 7hr 50 min. He plans to cross the North Sea on waterskis (360 miles) next year.

■ Prime Minister **Sir Anthony Eden**, arrives in Montego Bay, Jamaica, for a holiday 2¼ hrs early: His BOAC DC7 sets up a record for the Atlantic crossing. He'll stay at *Goldeneye* writer Ian (*James Bond*) Fleming's holiday home.

BRASHER'S GOLD

IT'S Gold Standard for Britain in the Melbourne Olympics . . . with an ecstatic Chris Brasher *(right)* **leading the way in the 3000m steeplechase. It is Britain's first track gold since 1932. He is followed onto the winner's rostrum by fencer Gillian Sheen** *(left)*, **a London dentist, who caps a memorable performance by beating Rumania's Olga Orban to claim Britain's first-ever fencing gold. Further successes come in the ring, with flyweight Terry Spinks** *(pictured, left)* **and lightweight Dick McTaggart and in the pool, where Judy Grinham wins the 100m backstroke in a record 72.9sec, the first swimming gold since 1924. The Duke of Edinburgh, who opens the Games, is made a Freeman of the city and later visits the Olympic village, dining with the athletes rather than at high table.**

■ Egypt will expel all British and French nationals within 10 days. The 13,000 British protected persons in Egypt will be allowed to take only £20 with them.

25 Sunday

The UN calls on Britain and France for the third time to **withdraw** troops from Egypt.
■ Many **garages shut** because of cuts in the petrol supply. RAC emergency services report many calls from motorists who have run out of petrol.
■ Between 10-12,000 volunteers help the police search Epping Forest for Boyd Fearon (3) who disappeared on November 15, but without success.

26 Monday

Dr John Bodkin Adams (57) is remanded on bail of £2,000 at Eastbourne, on 13 charges. Four charges relate to women patients. He must surrender his passport. *(See page 92)*.
■ The body of Boyd Fearon (3), missing from home in Romford since November 15, is found in 4ft of water in the River Rom.
■ Dance band leader **Tommy Dorsey** (51) is found dead at his home in Greenwich, Connecticut.

27 Tuesday

Peak-hour bus services in London will be kept up when **petrol rationing** begins on

December 17, but services outside peak hours will be cut.
■ **Egypt** announces harsh measures against 50,000 Jews. The only Jews who can remain are those who were Egyptian before 1900 – only 4 families qualify.

28 Wednesday

England beat Yugoslavia for the first time in 17yrs. **Stanley Matthews** sets up two of the three goals.
■ British artist Ben Nicholson, one of 99 candidates from 17 countries, wins the first international prize for painting awarded by the Guggenheim Foundation in Paris.

29 Thursday

Chris Brasher wins the 3000m steeple-chase in the Olympics *(see page 91)*.
■ The French government bans **homework** for children aged 6-11, starting on Jan. 1. Teachers must set aside an hour each day so the work can be done in class.
■ A 60-storey office **skyscraper** is to be built in New York on the east side of the Avenue of the Americas. It will be the tallest building in New York.

30 Friday

A channel 240ft wide has been cleared in Port Said harbour after a 400-ton floating crane is lifted and removed.
■ Some Negro children at school in Clinton, Tennessee now want transfers back to all-black schools, because of harassment from white schoolchildren.
■ London dental surgeon **Gillian Sheen** wins Olympic **gold** *(see page 91)*.
■ The **Nobel Prize** for Chemistry is awarded to British scientist Professor Sir Cyril Hinshelwood and a Russian for work on chemical kinetics. No Peace prize is awarded. Three Americans get the Physics prize for inventing and developing the transistor.

DECEMBER

1 Saturday

Britain wins two Olympic golds for boxing – **Dick McTaggart** and **Terry Spinks** *(see page 91)*.
■ There's a record entry of 6,417 dogs at the Birmingham Dog Show – the most popular breed is the miniature poodle. Best in Show is a cocker spaniel, Colinwood Silver Lariot.

2 Sunday
New Moon

Every available fireman and appliance in Leicester is called to fight a **fire** at silk throwsters Chapman, Frazer & Co. A large part of the factory is completely gutted – houses opposite had to be evacuated .
■ The Communist newspaper in **Budapest**, *Nepszabadsag*, admits there is not enough coal to heat schools and hospitals. Passive resistance to the government continues.

3 Monday

The **Duke of Edinburgh** is made the first Freeman of the city of Melbourne.
■ Percy Willis, the last survivor of the **Jameson Raid** of 1895, dies aged 80 in Nelspruit, Eastern Transvaal, South Africa. He was the guide to the force Dr Jameson led from Mafeking to aid a projected rising in Johannesburg in Transvaal.
■ **Selwyn Lloyd** *(left)* announces that British and French troops will be **with-drawn** immediately from the Suez zone.

4 Tuesday

The Lord Mayor of London's Hungarian relief fund reaches £1,145,000. There are large orders for a Christmas card by **Annigoni**, sold on behalf of the fund.
■ **Petrol** will go up by 1s. a gallon to 3s. 6d. Petrol prices will range from 5s. 6½d. – 6s. 5d.
■ America is demobilising its **pigeon** corps, because of progress in electronic communica-tion. The last 100 carrier pigeons will be